中级汉语口语

话 说 中 国

（修订版）

上 册

Speaking Chinese About China

(Revised Edition)

I

华语教学出版社
中国·北京

First Edition 1985
(First Published by Foreign Languages Press, Beijing, 1985)
Revised Edition   1989
Second Printing   1990
Third Printing   1995
Second Revision 2002

ISBN 7-80052-854-5
Copyright 2002 by Sinolingua
Published by Sinolingua
24 Baiwanzhuang Road, Beijing 100037, China
Tel: (86) 10-68995871 / 68326333
Fax: (86) 10-68326333
E-mail: hyjx@263.net
Printed by Beijing Foreign Languages Printing House
Distributed by China International
Book Trading Corporation
35 Chegongzhuang Xilu, P.O. Box 399
Beijing 100044, China

Printed in the People's Republic of China

原版编者

中国

北京大学	杜　荣　张起旺　赵燕皎
北京语言大学	杨石泉
北京外国语大学	姜林森

美国

Wellesley College （威斯理学院）	Helen T. Lin	（戴祝念）
	Ruby Y. C. Lam	（刘元珠）
	William W. Liu	（刘维汉）
	Theresa C. H. Yao	（郜树蕙）
	Micheal Crook	（柯马凯）

修订版编者

中国

北京大学	杜　荣

美国

Wellesley College （威斯理学院）	Ruby Y. C. Lam	（刘元珠）
	Theresa C. H. Yao	（郜树惠）

目　录

上　册

CONTENTS

I

前　言

1983 年 7 月，中美两国汉语教师在北京举行了"中美汉语教学讨论会"。双方经过认真讨论，同意就十三个教学与科研项目进行合作。《话说中国》就是其中的项目之一。

《话说中国》主要是为美国大学第二年汉语课编写的一部中级口语教材。课文题材包括中国地理、历史、政治、经济、社会、教育以及哲学思想等。教材按照内容分为七个单元，共二十课，分上下两册。读者通过学习，既可以提高汉语水平，也可以增进对中国文化的了解。

《话说中国》作为中美合编的教材，力求观点客观正确，内容丰富有趣，语言浅显活泼。这部教材不但适合美国大学学生使用，对于其他具有一定汉语基础的人也是适用的。

针对美国学生的具体情况，在体例上我们作了如下的安排：（1）课文有简体汉字、繁体汉字和汉语拼音三种形式。（2）考虑到中美划分汉语词类的习惯有所不同，注生词词性时，在力求统一的基础上分别列出两套注法，学生可以互相参阅。（3）无论是生词部分的例句还是句型练习中的例句，都有英语翻译，便于学生对比汉英两种语言，从而加深对汉语的理解。

学好一门外语，练习和实践是重要的一环。因此，根据我们的教学经验，选择学生一般感到不太容易掌握的常用句型，作为练习重点。除列举大量例句外，还尽力提供多样的练习，使学生通过练习学会这些常用句型的用法。（句型后所附的简短语法解释是供教师参考的，未加英语翻译。）每课还有内容相当丰富的翻译练习，帮助学生反复运用所学过的词语和句型。各课翻译练习的汉语答案都附在每单元后，这些答案也可用作汉译英的练习材料，对自学者尤其方便。此外，每单元后另有一篇副课文，分别介绍美国的地理、历史、政治、经济等，也是学生可能感兴趣的复习材料。

本书由中国方面担任主课文、句型练习和语法解释的编写工作，美国方面担任生词、翻译练习和副课文的编写工作。全书的每一部分都是经过双方协商确定的。

《话说中国》作为中美合作编写的第一部教材与读者见面，我们感到十分欣慰。由于编写时间仓促，这部教材肯定会有不少缺点和错误，欢迎读者批评指正。

本书承蒙北京大学王力教授题写书名，在此谨致谢忱。

美国芝加哥大学（University of Chicago）赵智超（George Chih Ch'ao Chao）教授和奥柏林学院（Oberlin College）徐凌志韫（Vivan Hsu）教授为副课文的编写提供了有关美国情况的资料，在此一并表示感谢。

编　者
1984 年 7 月

Preface

In July 1983 Chinese and American teachers of the Chinese language attended the Sino-U. S. Conference on Chinese Language Teaching held in Beijing. It was agreed at the conference that thirteen joint teaching and research projects be undertaken. *About China* is one of them.

About China is designed as an intermediate-level textbook of spoken Chinese for use in U. S. colleges in the second year. The subject matter includes Chinese geography, history, politics, economy, society, education, philosophy and other aspects of China. The texts, numbering twenty in all, are arranged in seven units according to the different topics, and will be published in two volumes. They will serve not only to raise readers' proficiency in Chinese but also to increase their knowledge of Chinese culture.

As a product of China-U. S. cooperation, *About China* strives for objectivity of outlook, wealth and variety of content and vividness and simplicity of language. It is hoped that the textbook will prove suitable for American college students as well as other learners with some basic knowledge of Chinese.

With requirements of American students in mind, we have made the following provisions: 1) The text is printed in simplified characters, nonsimplified characters and *pinyin*. 2) While specifying the parts of speech, we have also paid attention to the differences between Chinese and U. S. grammatical terminology, so two systems are offered and effort has been made to unify them as much as possible. 3) To facilitate comparison of the two languages, English translations are provided for all examples in the vocabulary and sentence-pattern sections.

Practice and exercises play an important part in the study of any foreign language, so we have selected as the core of our exercises some common sentence patterns that, in our experience, students seem to find hard to master. Besides a multitude of examples we have devised exercises of various kinds with a view to helping students master these patterns. (The brief grammar notes appended to the patterns are for the teacher's reference and are therefore not translated into English.) Each lesson also contains translation exercises calculated to give students practice in using new vocabulary and patterns. The Chinese answers to the exercises are given at the end of each unit. The answers can also be used for Chinese-English translation exercises—a feature that will prove especially useful to students studying Chinese on their own. Supplementary texts following each unit deal with U. S. geography, history, politics, economy, etc., and should prove of interest to students as review materials.

In the actual writing, the texts, pattern exercises and grammar notes were written by the Chinese team; while the vocabulary, translation exercises and supplementary texts were written by the American team. The final version of all parts was arrived at after consultation by both sides.

About China is the first joint enterprise of its kind undertaken by American and Chinese scholars. To make the experiment a success we welcome criticism and suggestions from all who use the textbook.

We wish to express our thanks to Professor Wang Li of Peking University for writing the Chinese title of our book, also to Professor Chih Ch'ao Chao of the University of Chicago and Professor Vivian Hsu of Oberlin College for providing materials on the United States to aid us in the writing of the supplementary texts.

The Authors

July 1984

修订版序

　　《话说中国》的上册和下册是先后在 1985 和 1987 年出版的，距今已经有十几年了。在这十几年中，中国的面貌不断发生新的变化，出版后不久，我们就已经感到书中有一些内容，尤其是下册中反映中国现实生活的一些内容，已经有些过时。但是，也许是因为这部中级口语教材的内容覆盖面较宽，语言还比较活泼，出版后的这些年仍然能够受到一些外国朋友的欢迎，到 1995 年已经再版了三次，这是我们始料所不及的。越是受到读者欢迎，就越感到有进一步修订的必要。遗憾的是本书的另一位主编美国威斯理学院的戴祝念（Helen T. Lin）教授在下册出版前就已经逝世，不能再和她一起商量，修订工作因而也就搁浅了。

　　1995 年我去美国和加拿大，看到一些学校仍在使用这部教材，当地一些教汉语的朋友在肯定这部教材的同时，也都建议我们能对其中已过时的内容进行必要的修订，当我提到自己已年老力衰恐无力完成时，有的朋友甚至表示愿意协助完成这项修订工作，这使我非常感动。回国后先后征询中美双方各位编者和华语教学出版社的意见，都表示同意修订，并商定修订工作由中国北京大学和美国威斯理学院两校的原编者合作进行，中国方面仍继续由我负责，美国方面由刘元珠（Ruby Y. C. Lam）和部树蕙（Theresa C. H. Yao）两位教授负责。双方经过磋商，决定美国方面负责各课翻译练习的修订，其余修订工作由中国方面负责。不巧的是，在修订工作开始后不久，北大的原编者张起旺和赵燕皎两位教授就先后被派往日本讲学，只剩下了我一个人，又因股骨头骨折卧床休养半年多，以致修订工作一拖再拖，直到最近才算完成。

　　此次修订对课文做了较大的改动，原上册的第 10 课和下册的第 1、3、7、9、10 课共六课都是重新编写的，原上册的第 8、9 两课和下册第 2 课也有较大的改动，其余各课都只对个别字句作必要的删改。随着课文的改动，生词和练习等等自然也都有很大变化。为了便于学习，修订本用 16 开本印行，全书内容也做了必要的缩减，主要有如下的改动：1. 不再分单元，原书各单元后所附副课文取消；2. 不再附列汉语拼音课文；3. 各课生词的词类不再分列两套标注法，只采用目前国内比较通行的词类系统标注。

　　在本书的修订本即将出版的时候，更加怀念已经逝世的美方主编戴祝念教授。我和她是在合作编写这部教材时才相识的，她那坦率热情的性格和幽默风趣的谈吐给我留下极其深刻的印象。她为编好这部教材倾注了极大的精力，我们之间为编写本书往返通信就有二十多次，直到她病重，还支撑着身体写信给我谈修改的意见，写出的字已不成字形，可见她是多么重视这部教材，遗憾的是她还没有来得及看到下册出版就与世长辞了。现在能有机会出版修订本，她如地下有知，当会含笑于九泉之下的。

杜　荣

2002 年 7 月

Preface to the Revised Edition

The first and second volumes of *About China* were originally published in 1985 and 1987, respectively. Nearly a decade has passed since then, and China has been constantly undergoing dramatic changes over this period of time. Shortly after the publication of the first edition, we already felt that certain parts of the book were out-of-date, especially the sections reflecting modern China in the second volume. However, students welcomed this intermediate-level book on spoken Chinese since we tried to provide a comprehensive course with lively everyday language. Until 1995, the first edition has been reprinted three times, and the popularity that it received has been beyond our expectations. This encouraged us and made us feel a more urgent need to produce a revised edition. Sadly, my co-author of this book, Professor Helen T. Lin of Wellesley College, passed away before the second volume of the first edition was published. Having lost her invaluable inputs, the plan to revise *About China* was put aside.

In 1995, I went on a trip to the United States and Canada, and saw that the first edition was still in use in quite a few schools. While the teachers using the book like it, they also expressed the need to have a more up-to-date edition. Initially, I had fear that I would not be able to carry through with a revision because of my age and poor health, but some of the teachers I met with offered to help me when they heard my doubts, and I was greatly touched by their interest and enthusiasm. When I came back to China after the trip, I contacted the editors of the book in China and the United States, as well as our publisher Sinolingua. Everyone was in favor of a revision, and it was decided that the project was to be carried out by the same team from Peking University and Wellesley College which helped produce the first edition. The project was headed by me in China, and by Ruby Y. C. Lam and Theresa C. H. Yao in the United States. After discussion, we decided that our U. S. collaborators would revise the translation exercises, while the Chinese team was responsible for the rest of the book. Unfortunately, two of the professors working with me, Zhang Qiwang and Zhao Yanjiao had to leave for lecturing trips in Japan shortly after the project began, so I was left on my own. Work was further delayed when I suffered a bone fracture due to a fall and had to be confined to bed for half a year. Despite these drawbacks, we have finally developed the second edition successfully.

This edition is a major revision of its predecessor. Six lessons were completely rewritten, including Lesson 10 in the original first volume, and Lessons 1, 3, 7, 9, and 10 in the original second volume. Lessons 8 and 9 in the first volume and Lesson 2 in the second volume also underwent major changes. For all other lessons, we only changed a few words and sentences as needed. Of course, vocabulary and exercise problems were updated along with the lessons as well. To facilitate reading, the second edition is published in the larger 16 format. The content of the book has also been condensed as follows: 1. the book is no longer separated into units, and the subordinate texts after each chapter in the first edition are eliminated; 2. *pinyin* text is removed; 3. the parts of speech of new vocabulary is now labeled by using a widely accepted system, instead of using two systems as before.

The publication of this new edition brings back to me memories of my former co-author Helen T. Lin who has left us years ago. We met each other while collaborating on the first edition of this book. Her frank and easy-going character and her sense of humor have impressed me deeply ever since I knew her. We have exchanged more than twenty letters overseas while working on this book, and she poured all her energy into it until the end. She continued writing to me with her suggestions on improving the book while she was critically ill, her handwriting was nearly ineligible by then. Sadly Helen did not live to see the second volume of the book in print. This book was extremely important to her, and now that a new edition has come out, I am sure that Helen will continue giving it her blessings.

Du Rong

July 2002

第1课

美丽的三大流域

美丽的三大流域

老师：同学们就要到中国去了。今天，我给大家介绍一下中国的地理环境。我想，你们一定很感兴趣。

中国在亚洲的东部，是亚洲的一个大国。中国不只是地方大，人口多，而且历史悠久，物产丰富，可讲的内容很多。从哪儿讲起呢？

约翰：老师，听说黄河是中国文化的摇篮，给我们讲讲黄河吧。

老师：好，就从黄河讲起。

请看墙上挂的地图：黄河在中国北部，由西往东，流过九个省，在山东流进大海，全长五千四百多公里。黄河是中国文化的摇篮，很久以前，中国人的祖先就在黄河流域生活、劳动，创造了中国的古代文化。黄河流域农业发达，是中国古代政治、经济、文化的中心。现在黄河两岸还有很多名胜古迹。

琳达：老师，为什么叫黄河呢？难道是黄色的吗？

汤姆：听说，黄河常常发生水灾。

老师：是的。黄河从黄土高原流过，带下来大量泥沙，河水变成了黄色，黄河的名字就是这么来的。因为河里的泥沙太多，所以常常发生水灾。但是，经过治理，现在黄河已经可以发电，可以灌溉了。

彼得：黄河是中国最长的河吗？

老师：不是，中国最长的河是长江。长江全长六千三百公里，是世界上第三长河。长江上游的四川盆地，土地肥沃，物产丰富，风景也不错。长江中下游有不少大大小小的湖，是有名的"鱼米之乡"。

玛丽：有本杂志上说，"上有天堂，下有苏杭"，这是什么意思？

老师：苏州、杭州这两个城市在长江下游，那儿不只是物产丰富，而且风景特别美。那么好的地方，只有天堂才能和它相比啊！

琳达： 太有意思了！

约翰： 这么说，长江流域是中国最好的地方了。

老师： 中国的好地方很多。东北大平原是一个重要的农业区，桂林山水就像画儿一样好看……这些以后再谈。请看地图：除了黄河、长江以外，在中国的南部还有一条大河，也是由西往东流，这就是珠江。珠江流域大部分是山地，下游比较平，雨水很充足，也是中国重要的农业区。广州是珠江流域政治、经济和文化的中心。中国的东南边靠着大海，海上交通对东南部的发展起了重要作用。

　　在这一课里，我们讲了中国的三大流域：黄河流域、长江流域和珠江流域。最后，请你们想一个问题：为什么黄河、长江、珠江都是由西往东流呢？你们好好研究一下中国地图，这个问题是不难回答的。

1. 地理 dìlǐ（名）

   geography

2. 环境 huánjìng（名）

   environment

   ○ 这儿的学习环境比别的学校好。

   This is a better place to study than other schools.

3. 感兴趣 gǎnxìngqù（动宾）

   be interested in

   兴趣 xìngqù（名）

   interest

   ○ 我对这件事不感兴趣。

   I am not interested in this.

   ○ 她对音乐有兴趣。

   She is interested in music.

4. (东) 部 (dōng) bù（名）

   (east) part

   ○ 美国西部有好几个大的国家公园。

   There are quite a few big national parks in the western part of the United States.

5. 不只……而且…… bùzhǐ... érqiě

   not only... but also

6. 人口 rénkǒu（名）

   population

7. 悠久 yōujiǔ（形）

   long, age-old

8. 物产 wùchǎn（名）

   products

9. 可 (讲) 的 kě (jiǎng) de

   worth mentioning

10. 从…… (讲) 起

   cóng... (jiǎng) qǐ

to begin with

11. 摇篮 yáolán（名）

cradle

12. 由……往…… yóu… wǎng…

from… to…

13. 祖先 zǔxiān（名）

ancestor

14. 流域 liúyù（名）

river valley

15. 创造 chuàngzào（动）

to create; creation

16. 古代 gǔdài（名）

ancient times

17. 农业 nóngyè（名）

agriculture

18. 发达 fādá（形）

developed, flourishing

○ 工业发达

The industry is well-developed.

○ 经济发达的国家

a country with well-developed economy

19. 经济 jīngjì（名）

economy, financial condition

○ 美国是经济发达的国家。

The United States has highly developed economy.

20. 中心 zhōngxīn（名）

center

○ 波士顿是美国的一个文化中心。

Boston is a cultural center of the United States.

21. 岸 àn（名）

bank, coast

22. 名胜古迹 míngshènggǔjì

scenic spots and historical sites

23. 难道……吗 nándào…… ma

Is it possible…?

24. 发生 fāshēng（动）

to occur

○ 那里年年发生水灾。

It floods there every year.

○ 这个故事发生在 1911 年。

This story took place in 1911.

25. 水灾 shuǐzāi（名）

flood

26. 大量 dàliàng（形）

large amount of

27. 泥沙 níshā（名）

mud and sand

28. 经过 jīngguò（动、名）

through；as a result of

○ 从北京坐火车去上海要经过南京。

From Beijing to Shanghai, the train goes through Nanjing.

○ 大家经过讨论，决定明天去长城。

After discussion, we decided to go to the Great Wall tomorrow.

○ 请你谈谈那件事情的经过。

Would you please talk about what has happened?

29. 治理 zhìlǐ（名、动）

control；to bring under control

○ 治理黄河

to bring the Yellow River under control

○ 治理国家

to rule the country

30. 发电 fādiàn（动宾）

to generate electricity

31. 灌溉 guàngài（动）

to irrigate

32. 上（中、下）游 shàng（zhōng，xià）yóu（名）

upper（middle，lower）reaches of a river

33. 盆地 péndì（名）

basin

34. 肥沃 féiwò（形）

fertile

35. 风景 fēngjǐng（名）

scenery

36. 大大小小 dàdàxiǎoxiǎo（形）

large and small, of all sizes

○ 大大小小的事都等着他来做。

He has to take care of all kinds of things.

37. 鱼米之乡 yúmǐzhīxiāng

land of fish and rice

38. 天堂 tiāntáng（名）

paradise

39. 像……一样 xiàng... yīyàng

to be like

40. 只有……才…… zhǐyǒu... cái...

only, only if ...

41. 和……相比 hé... xiāngbǐ

to compare with

42. 平原 píngyuán（名）

plain

43. 农业区 nóngyèqū（名）

agricultural area

区 qū（名）

area

44. 大部分 dàbùfen

greater part; most（of）

○ 大部分学生都做完了练习。

Most of the students have finished their homework.

45. 山地 shāndì（名）

mountainous region, hilly area

46. 平 píng（形）

flat, level

47. 雨水 yǔshuǐ（名）

rain, rainfall

48. 充足 chōngzú（形）

abundant, ample

49. 靠 kào（动）

near，by；to lean on

○ 我们家靠着黄河。

We live by the Yellow River.

○ 孩子靠在妈妈身上。

The child leans on her mother.

50. 交通 jiāotōng（名）

transportation

51. 起……作用 qǐ…zuòyòng

to have effect on

○ 你怎么说都起不了作用。

No matter what you say，it won't work.

52. 最后 zuìhòu（副、形）

lastly；last；in the end

○ 最后，大家都走了。

In the end everybody left.

○ 最后一个进来的人请关门。

The one who comes in last should close the door.

53. 研究 yánjiū（动、名）

to research，to consider

○ 你的意见很好，可是我们得再研究一下。

Your idea is very good，but we must give it further consideration.

○ 他现在研究什么？

What kind of research is he doing?

专 名

1. 亚洲	Yàzhōu	Asia
2. 黄河	Huánghé	the Yellow River
3. 山东	Shāndōng	Shandong Province
4. 黄土高原	Huángtǔ Gāoyuán	the Loess Plateau
5. 长江	Chángjiāng	the Yangtze River
6. 四川	Sìchuān	Sichuan Province
7. 苏（州）、杭（州）	Sū（zhōu）, Háng（zhōu）	Suzhou, Hangzhou
8. 东北	Dōngběi	the Northeast of China
9. 桂林	Guìlín	Guilin
10. 珠江	Zhūjiāng	the Pearl River
11. 广州	Guǎngzhōu	Guangzhou

语言点和练习

一、不只……而且……　not only… but also…

例句：

1. 北京不只是中国的政治中心，而且是文化中心。

   Beijing is not only China's political center, it is also its cultural center.

2. 现在，黄河不只可以灌溉，而且可以发电。

   Now the Yellow River can be used not only for irrigation, but also for generating electricity.

解释：

(All the Chinese explanations of grammar in this textbook are for the teachers' reference and are not translated into English.)

"不只""而且"都是连词，"不只……而且……"表示除了前边说的以外，还有进一层的意思。

练习：

1. 完成句子：
    (1) 她＿＿＿＿＿＿＿＿＿＿一个演员，＿＿＿＿＿＿＿＿＿＿作家。
    (2) 我们学校＿＿＿＿＿＿＿＿＿＿，而且很美。
    (3) 妹妹不只喜欢跳舞，＿＿＿＿＿＿＿＿＿＿。
    (4) 四川盆地不只＿＿＿＿＿＿＿＿＿＿＿＿＿＿＿＿，而且
       ＿＿＿＿＿＿＿＿＿＿＿＿＿＿。

2. 改写句子：
    (1) 中国地方大，人口也多。
    (2) 长江下游风景好看，物产也很丰富。
    (3) 她是我的妈妈，也是我的第一个老师。

二、可（讲）的（可＋V＋的）　worth V＋ing

例句：

1. 可说的　worth saying　　可去的　worth going to
   可看的　worth seeing　　可写的　worth writing about
2. 那个城市很古老，可看的地方很多。
   That is an ancient city with many places worth seeing.
3. 商店里东西不少，可买的不多。
   There are many goods in the store, but few worth buying.

解释：

"可＋V＋的"的结构可以放在名词前边作定语，也可以单独使用。单用时，作用相当于一个名词。如"可买的不多"意思是"可买的东西不多"。

练习：

1. 填空：
    (1) 北京是个有名的文化古城，＿＿＿＿＿＿＿＿＿＿很多。
    (2) 商店里东西很多，不过＿＿＿＿＿＿＿＿＿＿不多。
    (3) 长江中下游风景特别美，＿＿＿＿＿＿＿＿＿＿很多。
    (4) 展览会上＿＿＿＿＿＿＿＿＿＿不少。

2. 用"可讲的""可看的""可去的""可吃的"造句。

三、从……（讲）起（从……＋V＋起）　begin V＋ing from...

例句：

1. 请同学们从第 8 页看起。

   Please begin reading from page 8.

2. 就从去中国说起吧。

   Let's begin by talking about going to China.

3. 这是二十年前的事了，从哪儿说起呢？

   This happened twenty years ago, so where shall I begin talking about it?

4. 你想努力学习，那就从今天做起。

   If you want to study diligently, you should begin doing so today.

解释：

"从……＋V＋起"是说从哪儿（什么地方、什么时间、什么人或事）开始做的意见。"从哪儿说起呢？"是说头绪很多，不知道从哪儿开始说。

练习：

用"从……＋V＋起"改写句子：

(1) 我很想给你介绍一下美国的情况，可是不知道怎么开始说。

(2) 走进展览馆，老师让我们从东边开始看。

(3) 这件事要从十年以前开始讲。

(4) 这么多内容，我该从哪儿开始复习呢？

四、由……往……　from... to...

例句：

1. 中国的河流大部分都是由西往东流。

   Most rivers in China flow from west to east.

2. 那辆汽车由南往北开。

   That car was driven from south to north.

3. 骑自行车由山下往山上走特别困难。

   To ride a bicycle up the mountain is particularly difficult.

4. 水由桌子上往下流。

The water was running down the table.

解释：

"由……往……"也可以说"从……往……"。与"从……到……"不一样，"从……到……"是说从哪儿开始，到哪儿结束，可以指地方，也可以指时间。如"从北京到上海有两千多公里"，"从早到晚他都在忙"。"由……往……"是说从哪儿开始，向什么方向移动。如"由上往下流"，这种格式，只说地方，不说时间。

练习：

用"由……往……"或者"从……到……"填空：

(1) 坐飞机＿＿＿＿＿＿＿＿＿＿＿＿＿＿＿＿＿＿＿＿＿只要两个小时。

(2) 我们＿＿＿＿＿＿＿＿＿＿＿＿＿＿＿＿＿＿＿＿＿走。

(3) 这条河＿＿＿＿＿＿＿＿＿＿＿＿＿＿＿＿＿＿流。

(4) 他＿＿＿＿＿＿＿＿＿＿＿＿＿＿＿＿＿＿＿＿＿都很忙。

五、难道……（吗）？ Is it possible that...?

例句：

1. 这件事大家都知道，难道你不知道（吗）？

Everybody knows about it, is it possible that you don't?

2. 你已经去过三次中国，难道没有去过长城（吗）？

You have been to China three times, is it possible that you have never been to the Great Wall?

3. "大"字，难道你也不会念？

Can't you even read the character 大?

4. 以前，黄河发生的水灾难道还少吗？

Can it be possible that the Yellow River only flooded a few times in the past?

解释：

"难道"是副词，"难道……（吗）？"可以加强反问的语气。"难道"后边往往有否定词，形成"难道……不（没、没有）……吗？"的格式。

练习：

1. 用"难道……吗?"改写句子：
   (1) 男人能做到的事，女人也能做到。
   (2) 他是我们小时候的朋友，你一定认识。
   (3) 这么简单的问题，你应该懂。
   (4) 她是大学生，应该学过外语。

2. 用"难道"完成句子：
   (1) 我们是老同学，_____。
   (2) 这个电影很有名，_____。

3. 用"难道……吗?"造句。

六、只有……才……　　only if...

例句：

1. 只有努力，才能学好汉语。
   One can learn Chinese well only if one works hard at it.
2. 只有学好汉语，才能了解中国。
   Only when one learns Chinese well can one understand China.
3. 只有每天吃药，病才能好。
   One can get well only if one takes medicine every day.

解释：

"只有"是连词，表示唯一的条件，非此不可。后面多用副词"才"呼应。

练习：

完成句子：
(1) 只有你去请，_____。
(2) 只有每天复习，_____。
(3) _____，才能学习好。
(4) _____最了解孩子的习惯。
(5) 那个展览馆只有星期三_____。

七、和……相比　　to compare ... with

例句：

1. 美国和中国相比，土地面积差不多。

   The territory of the United States and the territory of China are approximately the same size.

2. 这条河小多了，不能和长江相比。

   This river is much smaller; it can't compare with the Yangtze River.

3. 和北京相比，广州的天气暖和多了。

   Compared with Beijing, Guangzhou has much warmer weather.

4. 他学习非常好，我不能和他相比。

   He does very well in his studies; I can't compare with him.

解释：

"和……相比"是指两个事物的比较，后面是比较的结果。"能和……相比"是说两个事物差不多；"不能和……相比"是说两个事物差别很大。

练习：

1. 用"和……相比"改写句子：

   (1) 学习上，我比他差多了。

   (2) 中国的人口分布，西部和东部很不一样。

   (3) 中国的历史比美国长。

   (4) 只有苏州杭州才跟天堂差不多。

2. 用"和……相比"造句。

八、像（跟、和）……一样（那样、这样） to be like

例句：

1. 她真好，像妈妈一样。

   She is nice, just like a mother.

2. 我们学校就像公园一样。

   Our campus is like a park.

3. 这里的山水跟画儿一样美。

   The scenery here is like a painting.

4. 我不像他那样努力。

   I don't work as hard as he does.

解释：

"像……一样"表示两个事物有共同点；"不像……那样"表示两个事物没有共同点。如果要特别指出那个共同点，就在"一样"后边说明。如例3、例4。

练习：

用"像（和、跟）……一样"完成句子：

(1) 姑娘像＿＿＿＿＿＿＿＿＿＿＿＿＿＿＿＿＿＿。

(2) 爸爸的身体＿＿＿＿＿＿＿＿＿＿＿＿＿＿＿好。

(3) 我每天学习，就像每天＿＿＿＿＿＿＿＿＿＿＿＿。

(4) 美国的密西西比河和中国的长江＿＿＿＿＿＿＿，都是世界上有名的长河。

九、除了……（以外）　except for...; besides

例句：

1. 除了小一点以外，这间房子很不错。

   This room is quite nice except that it is a bit small.

2. 除了下雨，他每天都练习长跑。

   Except when it rains, he practices long distance running every day.

3. 除了琳达以外，同学们都去过中国。

   All the students except Linda have been to China.

4. 除了中国以外，他还去过很多国家。

   He has been to many other countries besides China.

解释：

"除了……（以外）"表示不计算在内。如果在"除了……以外"，后边有"还"或"也"，则表示除了已经知道的外，还有别的。

练习：

1. 用"除了……以外"完成句子：

   (1) ＿＿＿＿＿＿＿＿＿＿＿＿＿＿＿＿，全班同学都来了。

   (2) 中国有三条大河，除了黄河以外，＿＿＿＿＿＿＿＿＿。

   (3) ＿＿＿＿＿＿＿＿＿＿＿＿＿＿，他哪儿也没去过。

2.用"除了……以外"改写句子:
   (1) 他每天上课,只有星期天才出去玩。
   (2) 你懂汉语,你们家还有懂汉语的吗?
   (3) 中国不只是长江下游好,中国的好地方很多。

十、对……起……作用 to have effect on

例句:
   1.黄河对中国文化的发展起过重要作用。
   The Yellow River had important effect on Chinese culture.
   2.老师的话对他不起作用。
   What the teacher says does not have any effect on him.
   3.这种药对我的病不起作用。
   This medicine is not effective in treating my disease.
   4.复习对他的学习起了很大作用。
   Reviewing the old lessons is proved beneficial to his study.

解释:
   一般有三种格式: 1) A 对 B 起作用。2) A 对 B 起……作用。3) A 对 B 不起作用。

练习:
   1.用"起……作用"完成句子:
   (1) 交通的发达_____。
   (2) 现在,黄河对 _____ 起着
   _____作用。
   (3) _____对我_____不起作用。
   2.用"对……起……作用"造句。

听力练习

(听录音,听力问题见本书附录)

回答问题

1. 为什么有人说黄河是中国文化的摇篮？
2. 黄河以前为什么常常发生水灾？
3. 黄河这个名字是怎么来的？
4. 长江重要吗？为什么？
5. 鱼米之乡是什么地方？为什么叫鱼米之乡？
6. 请你说一说长江上游的情况。
7. 请你讲一讲中国的三大流域。
8. 中国物产最丰富的地方在哪儿？
9. "上有天堂，下有苏杭"这句话的意思是什么？
10. 请你介绍一下你们国家的地理环境。

翻译练习

（英译汉，答案见本书附录）

1. geographical environment
2. to speak about the geography of China
3. to be interested in history
4. the products from central Asia
5. Products are relatively abundant.
6. a magazine that is rich in content
7. a long history
8. a civilization of long standing
9. Read from Lesson One.
10. to begin with the culture of the Yellow River valley
11. The Yangtze River also flows from west to east.
12. the population of the whole nation
13. The school has five thousand students in all.
14. to study ancient Chinese history

15. Agriculture is more developed than industry.
16. to develop agriculture in the Sichuan Basin
17. The cities along the river have highly developed industry.
18. to turn into a political center
19. to visit scenic spots and historical sites
20. Something important occurred.
21. after studying hard
22. The middle reaches go through three provinces.
23. to bring the Yellow River under control
24. The Yangtze River can generate electricity.
25. to irrigate agricultural areas
26. large plain with fertile land
27. most of the tributaries of the river
28. cities of all sizes
29. The mountainous region has an ample amount of rainfall.
30. just like paradise
31. near the land of fish and rice
32. Marine transportation is well developed.
33. to the development of transportation
34. had great effect on the development of economy
35. Not only is the land fertile, the scenery is also beautiful.
36. There are so many scenic spots and historical sites worth seeing in China.
37. Do you mean to say that the Yellow River can still flood after it has been brought under control?
38. This was how the ancestors of the Americans lived.
39. Did ancient Chinese culture develop from the North to the South?
40. That is how it got the name of "cultural cradle".
41. Only when marine transportation is developed, can industry flourish.
42. Most of the rivers flow from west to east.
43. The ample amount of rainfall had great effect on the development of agriculture.
44. The scenery of Suzhou and Hangzhou is rare indeed.
45. In addition to being a political center, Beijing is also a cultural center.
46. There are many topics in Chinese culture that are not only worth studying, but also very interesting.

47. Lastly, I will read them over again beginning from the first sentence.
48. Do you mean that the Loess Plateau cannot be irrigated?
49. Because the water in the Yellow River contains a large amount of mud and sand, the color of the water has turned yellow.
50. China has quite a few agricultural areas like the one in the Northeast.

第 2 课

辽阔的国土

辽阔的国土

老师：请你们先回答我上次提出的问题：中国的三条大河黄河、长江、珠江为什么都是由西往东流呢？

约翰：因为中国西边高，东边低。

老师：对，"人往高处走，水往低处流"嘛！中国地形的特点就是西高东低。西边不是高原，就是山地；东边多半是平原。

请大家看地图：这一大块地方是青藏高原，世界最高峰——珠穆朗玛峰就在这高原的南边。谁要是登上这座高峰，谁就是世界上站得最高的人了。

琳达：我想试试。

约翰：那真是"人往高处走"了。小心摔下来！

老师：你们看：这儿是新疆，这儿是内蒙古，这一带大部分也是高原和山地。

汤姆：高原上的人怎么生活呢？

老师：那里耕地不多，人们主要靠放牧生活。

琳达：听说新疆和内蒙古的草原很美呢！

老师：是啊，"天苍苍，野茫茫，风吹草低见牛羊"，这首民歌说的就是草原的自然景色。

彼得：太美了！有机会我一定去那儿看看。难道一年四季都那么好看吗？

玛丽：你也不想想，那儿是中国的北方，冬天比这儿冷多了。老师，我说的对不对？

老师：是这样。中国北方，气候干旱少雨，冬天冷，夏天热；南方气候温和，雨水充足，更适合发展农业。由于气候不同，南北方的农作物也不一样：南方主要是水稻，北方主要是小麦。

汤姆：中国的矿产多不多？

老师：中国的矿产资源很丰富。北方是中国的能源基地，煤和石油都相当多，对工业的发展起着重要作用。因为受气候、地形和物产的影响，中国人口的分布很不平均。你们想想看，中国什么地方人口最多？

同学们：东部。

老师：为什么呢？

约翰：因为那儿气候温和，土地肥沃。

琳达：而且物产丰富，当然人口就多了。

老师：回答得很好。中国的大城市，像北京、天津、南京、上海、广州等都在东部。

琳达：老师，听说台湾的人口也不少。你能给我们讲讲台湾吗？

老师：当然可以。中国东南沿海有许多大大小小的海岛，其中最有名的就是台湾。台湾离中国大陆只有一百多公里，面积有三万五千七百八十平方公里。台湾虽然不大，但是物产十分丰富，风景也很美，自古以来就是中国的一个宝岛。

玛丽：中国人口那么多，有多少民族呢？

老师：中国是一个多民族的国家，有五十多个民族，分布在全国各地。汉族人口最多，大约占全国人口的百分之九十四，主要集中在东部和南部。其他民族人数比较少，叫少数民族，主要分布在西南、西北、东北等地区。中国的民族虽然多，却很团结。在这一课里，除了中国的地形、气候、物产以外，我们还谈了人口和民族的分布情况，讲的内容都非常简单。详细的情况还要靠同学们自己去看，去了解。

生　　词

1. **辽阔** liáokuò（形）

   vast

2. **人往高处走** rén wǎng gāochù zǒu

   The nature of people is to move up in life, just as the

   水往低处流 shuǐ wǎng dīchù liú

   nature of water is to flow downward.

3. **地形** dìxíng（名）

   topography

4. **特点** tèdiǎn（名）

   characteristics

5. **高原** gāoyuán（名）

   plateau

6. **峰** fēng（名）

   peak

   高峰 gāofēng（名）

   high peak

   山峰 shānfēng（名）

   mountain peak

7. **登** dēng（动）

   to climb（up）

   ○ 登山运动

   mountain climbing

   ○ 登上万里长城

   to climb the Great Wall

8. **试试** shìshi（动）

   to try

9. **小心** xiǎoxīn（形、动）

   careful；to watch out

   ○ 写字的时候得小心，别写错。

   When you write, please be careful and don't make mistakes.

   ○ 小心火车！

Watch out for the train!

○ 他办事特别小心。

He is extremely prudent in his work.

10. 摔 shuāi（动）

to fall (down)

○ 孩子摔倒了。

The child fell down.

○ 慢慢上，别摔下来。

Go up slowly, or you might fall down.

11. 一带 yīdài（名）

area, region

12. 耕地 gēngdì（名）

arable land

13. 靠……生活 kào... shēnghuó

to depend on... for a living

14. 放牧 fàngmù（动）

to herd

15. 草原 cǎoyuán（名）

grassland

16. 天苍苍，野茫茫，
风吹草低见牛羊。

Tiān cāngcāng,

"Blue, blue, the sky,

yě mángmáng,

Vast, vast, the field,

fēng chuī cǎo dī

The grasses are blown,

xiàn niú yáng.

The cattle are shown."

17. 首 shǒu（量）

(measure word for poems)

18. 民歌 míngē（名）

folksong

19. 自然 zìrán（名）

nature

20. 景色 jǐngsè（名）

scenery

21. 机会 jīhuì（名）

opportunity, chance

○ 这个机会很好。

This is a very good opportunity.

○ 这是个学习中文的好机会。

This is a good chance to learn Chinese.

22. 干旱 gānhàn（形）

dry

23. 气候 qìhòu（名）

climate

24. 温和 wēnhé（形）

mild（weather, temperament）

○ 南方的气候比北方温和。

The climate is milder in the south than in the north.

○ 那个护士很温和，病人都喜欢她。

That nurse has a mild temperament and all the patients like her.

25. 适合 shìhé（动）

suitable

26. 由于 yóuyú（介）

due to, because

27. 农作物 nóngzuòwù（名）

agricultural produce, crops

28. 水稻 shuǐdào（名）

paddy-rice

29. 小麦 xiǎomài（名）

wheat

30. 矿产 kuàngchǎn（名）

minerals

31. 资源 zīyuán（名）

natural resources

○ 人是很重要的资源。

People are important resources.

32. 能源 néngyuán（名）

26

energy resources

○ 能源问题对每个国这都很重要。

The energy problem is important to every country.

33. **基地** jīdì （名）

base

34. **煤** méi （名）

coal

35. **石油** shíyóu （名）

petroleum

36. **影响** yǐngxiǎng （动、名）

to have an effect on; influence

○ 农作物受气候的影响。

Crops are affected by the weather.

○ 吸烟影响了他的健康。

His health has been affected by smoking.

37. **分布** fēnbù （动）

to be distributed

38. **平均** píngjūn （形、动）

average; even

○ 她们的平均年龄只有二十岁。

Their average age is only twenty.

○ 每班平均有十个学生。

Each class averages ten students.

○ 每个国家能源基地的分布都不平均。

The distribution of energy bases is uneven in all countries.

39. **当然** dāngrán （副）

of course

○ 你去吗? Are you going?

当然去。Of course.

○ 中国南方土地肥沃、雨水充足，人口当然比北方多了。

South China has fertile soil and plenty of rain，so of course its population is larger than that of north China.

40. **沿海** yánhǎi （名）

coast; coastal

41. **海岛** hǎidǎo （名）

island

42. 其中 qízhōng（名）

in which, among which（as an adjunct, with an antecedent previously stated）

○ 我们班二十个学生，其中有一半是从美国东部来的。

We have twenty students in our class, half of whom come from the eastern part of the United States.

○ 中国风景美的地方很多，其中苏杭两个城市最美。

In China, there are many places with beautiful scenery and among them, Suzhou and Hangzhou are the most beautiful.

43. 大陆 dàlù（名）

continent, mainland

44. 面积 miànjī（名）

area

45. 平方公里 píngfānggōnglǐ

square kilometer

公里 gōnglǐ（量）

kilometer

46. 自古以来 zìgǔyǐlái

since ancient times

47. 宝岛 bǎodǎo（名）

treasure island

48. 大约 dàyuē（副）

approximately, generally

○ 现在大约是八点钟。

It's about 8 o'clock now.

○ 从北京到广州大约有两千公里。

It is about 2000 kilometers from Beijing to Guangzhou.

49. 占 zhàn（动）

to constitute

50. 百分之…… bǎifēnzhī…

percentage

○ 城市人口占全国人口的百分之六十。

Urban population constitutes 60 percent of the entire population.

○ 中国人百分之九十以上是汉族。

Over 90 percent of the Chinese population are of Han nationality.

51. 集中 jízhōng（动）

    to concentrate

○ 中国的大城市集中在东部和南部。

Most of the big cities in China are located in the East and the South.

52. 其他 qítā（代）

    other

○ 谁还有其他的问题？

Who has other questions?

53. 人数 rénshù（名）

    number of people

54. 少数 shǎoshù（名）

    minority

55. 等 děng（代）

    and others, etc.

    等等 děngděng（代）

    and others, etc.

○ 像北京、天津等中国北方的城市，冬天都下雪。

Cities of northern China such as Beijing, Tianjin, etc. all have snow in winter.

○ 这种花有红、白、黄、蓝等等颜色。

This kind of flower comes in red, white, yellow, blue and other.

56. 地区 dìqū（名）

    area, region

57. 却 què（副）

    yet, but

○ 那个地区虽然农业不发达，矿产却很丰富。

The agriculture of that region is not developed, but it is rich in minerals.

58. 详细 xiángxì（形）

    detailed

专名

1. 青藏高原	Qīngzàng Gāoyuán	the Qinhai-Tibet Plateau
2. 珠穆朗玛峰	Zhūmùlǎngmǎ Fēng	Mount Qomolangma（Mount Everest）
3. 新疆	Xīnjiāng	Xinjiang
4. 内蒙古	Nèiměnggǔ	Inner Mongolia
5. 天津	Tiānjīn	Tianjin
6. 南京	Nánjīng	Nanjing
7. 台湾	Táiwān	Taiwan
8. 汉族	Hànzú	the Han nationality

语言点和练习

一、嘛 used with a tone of assurance

例句：

1. 不用谢，这是应该的嘛！

   Don't mention it; this is what I should do.

2. 有问题问老师嘛！

   Go and ask the teacher if you have any questions.

3. 台湾自古以来就是中国的嘛！

   Taiwan has belonged to China since ancient times.

4. A：他怎么没有来？

   Why didn't he come?

   B：他有病嘛！

   He was sick.

解释：

"嘛"是语气助词，放在句子后面，表示肯定的语气，有"本来就是这样，本来就应该这样"的意思。

练习：

1. 区别"吗"和"嘛"，想想每组里的两个句子有什么不同。

(1) 这是应该的吗？　　这是应该的嘛！

(2) 他有病吗？　他有病嘛！

(3) 她早来了吗？　　她早来了嘛！

2．用"嘛"回答问题：

(1) 你怎么认识她的？

(2) 你为什么那么喜欢中文书？

(3) 为什么中国人口集中在东部？

(4) 草原上的人为什么靠放牧生活？

二、不是……就是……　either... or...

例句：

1．这几天天气很不好，不是刮风就是下雨。

The weather has been very bad recently; if it isn't raining, it's blowing.

2．这本书不是你的就是我的，不会是别人的。

This book is either yours or mine; it cannot belong to anybody else.

3．学生们从早到晚都在学习，不是上课就是做练习。

Students study from morning till night; if they aren't attending class they are doing homework.

解释：

"不是……就是……"意思是非 A 即 B，不会是别的。A 与 B 必须是同类词语。

练习：

1．用"不是……就是……"改写句子：

(1) 要不你去，要不我去，别人是不去的。

(2) 住在这个地方的人只有汉族和回族。

(3) 那里只有高原和山地。

(4) 他每天总是看书，写文章。

2．用"不是……就是……"回答问题：

(1) 这枝铅笔是谁的？

(2) 那儿的天气怎么样？

(3) 中国西部的地形有什么特点？

（4）星期天你做什么？

3. 用"不是……就是……"造句。

三、谁……谁……　whoever...

例句：

1. 谁先到谁买票。

   Whoever gets there first will buy the tickets.

2. 谁想好了谁回答我的问题。

   Whoever is ready will answer my question.

3. 大家都想去，谁去谁高兴，谁不去谁不高兴。

   Everybody wants to go; whoever does will be happy, those who don't won't.

4. 这件事谁干的谁知道。

   Whoever did it must know it.

解释：

"谁"原来是疑问代词，在"谁……谁……"的格式里，"谁"表示任指。前后两个"谁"指的是同一个（或一些）人。

练习：

1. 用"谁……谁……"改写句子：

   （1）先来的那个人开窗子。

   （2）会的人先回答。

   （3）学习好的去中国。

   （4）喜欢去的人都可以去。

2. 用"谁……谁……"完成句子：

   （1）谁登上珠穆朗玛峰_____。

   （2）谁会唱歌_____。

   （3）_____谁打扫
       屋子。

   （4）_____谁回答。

   （5）明天晚上有音乐会，谁愿意去_____。

   （6）这枝笔真好，谁看见_____。

四、动词重叠 + （看）　 to try

例句：

1. 请你试试这件衣服。

   Please try on the clothes.

2. 请你说说中国的地理环境。

   Please talk about the geographical environment of China.

3. 晚上，我听听广播、看看画报、写写汉字，念念课文，过得很有意思。

   I listened to the radio, read some pictorials, practiced writing Chinese characters, and studied the texts; I have had a wonderful evening.

4. A：你能登上这座山吗？

   Can you climb this mountain?

   B：我想试试（看）。

   I would like to try.

5. 你们想想（看），为什么中国的大城市集中在东南部？

   Just think it over, why are the big cities in China all loctated in the southeastern part of the country?

解释：

汉语动词可以重叠，表示动作时间短暂、随便，或有尝试的意思。动词重叠后若加上"看"字（多见于单音动词），则只有尝试的意思。"看"后需要停顿。这种用法常用于口语。

练习：

1. 组织词组（短语）：

   听听_____　　写写_____　　试试_____

   说说_____　　念念_____　　讲讲_____

   打打_____　　想想_____　　等等_____

2. 用动词重叠或者动词重叠加"看"完成句子：

   (1) 约翰：大夫，我有点发烧。

   　　大夫：_____。

   (2) 每天_____汉字_____课文，进步一定很快。

   (3) 你能回答这个问题吗？　　让我_____。

   (4) 难道你不记得他叫什么名字了吗？你再_____。

五、靠…… to rely on...

例句：

1. 中国的东南靠着大海。

   The southeastern part of China is by the coast.

2. 孩子靠在妈妈身上。

   The child is leaning on her mother.

3. 那儿的人靠种地生活。

   The people there live on farming.

4. 学习主要靠自己努力，不能只靠别人帮助。

   Learning mainly relies upon one's own effort, not just on help from somebody else.

解释：

"靠"是动词，有三个意思：一是作"接近"讲，如例1；二是倚靠的意思，如例2；三是依靠的意思，如例3、4。

练习：

1. 用"靠（着）"完成句子：

   (1) 美国东部＿＿＿＿＿＿＿＿＿＿＿＿＿＿＿。

   (2) 他的身体＿＿＿＿＿＿＿＿＿＿＿＿＿＿＿。

   (3) ＿＿＿＿＿＿＿＿＿＿＿＿＿＿＿，她才找到工作。

   (4) 我们的宿舍＿＿＿＿＿＿＿＿＿＿＿。

2. 用"靠"的三个不同意思造句。

3. 回答问题：

   (1) 学习主要靠什么？

   (2) 美国西部山区的人主要靠什么生活？

六、由于 owing to，as a result of

例句：

1. 由于地形不同，东部和西部的气候很不一样。

   Owing to the difference in topography, the weather in the east and west is not the same.

2．由于身体不好，他没来上课。

He did not go to school because of sickness.

3．由于大家都知道的原因，两国的关系不太好。

Because of the reason that is publicly known, the relationship between the two countries is deteriorating.

4．东部人口集中，是由于那里气候好、物产丰富。

As a result of good weather and abundance in production, the eastern part is densely populated.

解释：

"由于"表示原因，它常常放在主语前面，但也可以出现在"是"的后面。

练习：

1．改写句子，用"由于"把两个句子连起来：

(1) 昨天下雨。我们没去公园。

_____。

(2) 中国地形的特点是西高东低。黄河、长江都是由西往东流。

_____。

(3) 我对音乐不感兴趣。我没参加昨天的音乐会。

_____。

2．用"由于"完成句子：

(1) 人们说苏杭跟天堂一样，是_____。

(2) _____，每次考试都考得不错。

(3) _____，草原上的人靠放牧生活。

七、像　such as

例句：

1．中国的好地方很多，像苏州、杭州、桂林、青岛等都是游览的好地方。

There are many good places for sightseeing in China, such as Suzhou, Hangzhou, Guilin, and Qingdao.

2．汉字也有非常简单的，像"人、口、手、山、水"等。

Chinese characters can also be simple, such as the words for person, mouth, hand, mountain, water and so on.

3. 他会很多种外语，像汉语、日语、法语等都说得很好。

He speaks fluently in many foreign languages, such as Chinese, Japanese and French.

解释：

"像……（一样）"有"相像"的意思（第一课）。不加"一样"有时还有"例如"的意思（本课）。

练习：

1. 用"像"完成句子：
   (1) 我去过很多国家，_____。
   (2) 中国电影我看过不少，_____ 我都看过。
   (3) 我有很多中国朋友，_____。
   (4) 中国的大河都是由西往东流，_____。
   (5) 中国的大城市_____我都去过。

2. 用"像……一样"或者"像……"改写句子：
   (1) 孩子的脸红得跟苹果差不多。
   (2) 世界上有几条相当长的河，例如长江、密西西比河、尼罗河、亚马逊河都是世界有名的长河。
   (3) 桂林山水和画儿差不多。
   (4) 只有苏杭才能和天堂相比。
   (5) 带"氵"的汉字都跟水有关系，例如"河、江、湖、海"等。

八、虽然……但是（可是）/却……　although… /yet…

例句：

1. 草原地方虽然大，但是可耕种的土地不多。

Given that the grassland is vast, the arable land is limited.

2. 父亲虽然去过很多次中国，但是一句汉语也不会说。

My father has been to China many times, but he cannot speak Chinese at all.

3. 我虽然喜欢音乐，可是不会唱歌。

Although I like music, I cannot sing.

36

4. 虽然是夏天，山上却很冷。

Although it is summer, it is cold on the mountains.

5. 这孩子虽然年龄不大，懂的事情却不少。

Given that he is a child, he knows a lot of things.

解释：

"虽然A但是（可是）/却B"表示让步，承认A是事实，但B并不因此而不成立。"虽然"用在前一个小句，可在主语前，也可在主语后。后一小句中常有"但是、可是、却"等与之相呼应。"却"不能用在主语前。

练习：

1. 完成句子：

(1) 他虽然只学了半年汉语，_____。

(2) 虽然他不想去，_____。

(3) 汉字_____，却很有意思。

(4) _____，可是没有去过桂林。

2. 指出下列句子的错误，并改写：

(1) 老师讲得虽然简单，但是我们不感兴趣。

(2) 虽然下着大雨，却她们玩得很高兴。

(3) 这孩子虽然小，懂得事情却很少。

(4) 那个村子虽然很小，但是大家都不知道。

九、（自、从、自从）……以来　since

例句：

1. 自古以来，台湾就是中国的一个省。

Taiwan has been part of China since ancient times.

2. 从去年九月以来，我已经收到二十封家信。

Since September of last year, I have already received twenty letters from home.

3. 自从学习汉语以来，他每天都听汉语广播。

Ever since he studied Chinese, he has listened to the Chinese broadcast every day.

4. 新中国成立以来，发生了很大变化。

Ever since the founding of new China, great changes have taken place.

解释：

"自……以来"、"从……以来"、"自从……以来"、"……以来"表示从那个时候直到现在这段时间。

练习：

    1．用"（自、从、自从）……以来"完成句子：

       （1）自古以来，_____。

       （2）从学习开始以来_____。

       （3）自生病以来_____。

       （4）_____，我每天锻炼身体。

       （5）这个学校自成立以来_____。

    2．用"自……以来"造句。

听力练习

（听录音，听力问题见本书附录）

回答问题

    1．中国地形有什么特点？它跟中国的三大流域有什么关系？

    2．世界第一高峰在哪儿？叫什么名字？

    3．请你简单介绍一下新疆和内蒙古的情况。

    4．中国北方和南方的气候有什么不同？对农业发展有什么影响？

    5．为什么中国东南部的人口比其他的地区多？

    6．中国有些什么矿产资源？主要分布在什么地方？

    7．中国的大城市为什么都集中在沿海一带？

    8．请你简单地介绍一下台湾的情况。

    9．请你详细地说一说中国人口分布的情况。

  10．请你谈谈中国为什么是一个多民族的国家。

  11．你的国家地形有什么特点，请简单介绍一下。

12. 美国是一个多民族的国家吗？主要有哪些民族？

13. 多民族国家的文化有什么特点？

14. 你们国家的能源基地在哪儿？有什么主要的矿产资源？

15. 你们国家的人口分布平均吗？受到什么影响？

翻译练习

（英译汉，答案见本书附录）

1. high in the west and low in the east

2. to flow from west to east

3. the characteristics of the terrain

4. to introduce the characteristics of Chinese culture

5. mostly plateaus

6. Most of them lived along the Yellow River.

7. to promote the sport of mountain climbing

8. to climb on top of the highest mountain peak

9. to try to ask questions in Chinese

10. Be careful not to write the characters wrong.

11. to be careless and fall off the chair

12. to rely on livestock raising for a living

13. mainly rely on exercise

14. a folksong that tells of the scenery of the grassland

15. to have no chance to visit

16. The sceneries of the four seasons are all different.

17. The weather in the summer is dry with little rainfall.

18. warm as spring

19. therefore not suitable for the students to use

20. The grassland is suitable for raising cattle.

21. The weather is very dry and not suitable for the development of agriculture.

22. because the agricultural products are different

23. for its richness in mineral deposits

24. to develop the energy basis

25. the petroleum fields in the west
26. to be influenced by the distribution of the population
27. to influence the development of industry
28. evenly distributed in every province
29. unevenly distributed
30. Folksongs are not only pretty, but also easy to learn.
31. Of course it is influenced by the weather.
32. cities along the sea coast
33. islands of all sizes
34. Among those, Taiwan is the largest.
35. 90 percent of the people
36. The rainfall is very abundant.
37. a country with many nationalities
38. The Han nationality constitutes about 94%.
39. to constitute about 3/10
40. to concentrate along the sea coast regions
41. The number of people is larger than that in other cities.
42. the areas where the national minorities are distributed
43. The content is simple and clear.
44. The main agricultural product of most countries is either rice or wheat.
45. Those who want to go to China to study must thoroughly understand China's situation.
46. Don't rely on others; one must first try to do it oneself.
47. Because energy resources are not abundant, industry is not well developed.
48. The coastal areas not only have dense population and convenient transportation, but also have highly developed industries.
49. There are more than a thousand students in that school; is it possible that there isn't even one Chinese?
50. Since ancient times, Taiwan has always been an important island off the China coast.

第 3 课

愉快的旅游

愉快的旅游

亲爱的老师：

　　您好！

　　今年暑假，我和几个同学参加了一个旅行团到中国来了。我们游览了许多地方，觉得特别有意思。您一定很想知道我们这次旅游的情况吧？

　　我们是乘飞机到北京的。北京是中国的首都，也是一座有三千年历史的文化古城。北京做过元、明、清等朝代的国都，所以名胜古迹特别多。

　　第二天早上，我们就去长城了。登上长城一看，山峰一座连着一座，长城就建筑在这些高山上，非常雄伟壮观。听说长城有一万多里长，真了不起！

　　在北京，我们参观了天安门广场，还游览了故宫和颐和园。那里的宫殿，都很有中国古代建筑的特色。后来，我们又参观了北京大学和其他一些地方，就坐火车到西安去了。

　　西安跟北京一样，也是一座有名的文化古城。从公元前十一世纪开始，西安做过周、秦、汉、唐等朝代的国都，可参观的名胜古迹相当多，其中最有名的是秦始皇兵马俑博物馆。

　　在西安玩了三天，我们又坐火车到了重庆。重庆是长江上游的一座山城，不但风景优美，而且在经济上占有重要的地位。

　　重庆的交通比较方便。从重庆上船，顺流而下，第二天早上就进入了长江三峡。三峡两岸的山峰很陡，江面又窄又曲折，水流得很急，船也走得很快。有几次，我们的船好像就要撞到山上了，可是一拐弯儿，又从山旁边开了过去。这时候，我想起您教过的两句唐诗："两岸猿声啼不住，轻舟已过万重山。"

　　船到武汉，我们住了一夜；第二天，就坐飞机到了上海。上海是中国最大的城市，也是东南沿海最大的港口，工商业非常发达。我们住的旅馆在市中心，那儿一天到晚都很热闹。

苏州离上海不远，从上海坐火车，只要一个多小时就到了。苏州是有名的"园林之城"，那里的园林小巧别致，各有特色。纽约市博物馆的"明轩"，就是按照苏州的一个园林建造的。

杭州是另外一种景色。西湖三面环山，风景秀丽。听说宋代一位诗人，把西湖比作一位漂亮的女子——西施，所以西湖也叫西子湖。自古以来，杭州就是有名的风景区，而且有许多民间传说和历史故事。在杭州，我买了两盒龙井茶，等回国以后，我们见面的时候，再一边品尝，一边细谈吧！

这次，我亲眼看到中国各方面的情况，进一步了解了中国，提高了研究中国文化的兴趣。对您在这方面的教导，我表示衷心的感谢。

祝您健康！

您的学生　琳达

七月十二日

生　词

1. **亲爱的** qīnàide（形）

    dear

2. **暑假** shǔjià（名）

    summer vacation

3. **旅行团** lǚxíngtuán（名）

    tour group

4. **游览** yóulǎn（动）

    to go sightseeing

5. **觉得** juéde（动）

    to think, to feel

    ○ 我觉得很热。

    I feel very hot.

    ○ 我觉得这是一个好机会。

    I think this is a good chance.

6. **朝代** cháodài（名）

    dynasty

    朝 cháo（名）

    dynasty

    代 dài（名）

    dynasty, historical period

7. **国都** guódū（名）

    national capital

8. **连（着）** lián（zhe）（动）

    to connect; in succession

    ○ 那个地方山连着山，水连着水，风景很美。

    The scenery there is very beautiful with many mountains, lakes and rivers.

    ○ 上个星期连着下了三天雨。

    Last week it rained for three days without a break.

9. **建筑** jiànzhù（动、名）

    to build, to construct; building, architecture

44

○ 那座古城是什么朝代建筑的？

During which dynasty was that ancient city built?

○ 北京有许多古代建筑。

There are many ancient buildings in Beijing.

10. **雄伟** xióngwěi（形）

grand

11. **壮观** zhuàngguān（形）

grand, magnificent

12. **了不起** liǎobuqǐ（形）

terrific, wonderful

○ 他觉得自己了不起。

He thinks that he himself is wonderful.

○ 他是个了不起的人。

He is remarkable.

13. **广场** guǎngchǎng（名）

public square

14. **宫殿** gōngdiàn（名）

palace

15. **后来** hòulái（副）

later on, afterwards

○ 他学了三年汉语，后来又学了一年历史。

He studied Chinese for three years and then he also studied history for one year.

16. **特色** tèsè（名）

special feature, characteristics

17. **公元** gōngyuán（名）

A. D.; the Christian era

18. **世纪** shìjì（名）

century

19. **博物馆** bówùguǎn（名）

museum

20. **相当** xiāngdāng（副）

considerably, quite

○ 他的妻子相当漂亮。

His wife is quite pretty.

○ 中国南方的气候冬天相当温和。

In winter the weather in southern China is quite warm.

21. 地位 dìwèi（名）

position, status

22. 不但……而且…… bùdàn…érqiě…

not only... also

23. 优美 yōuměi（形）

beautiful, graceful

24. 顺流而下 shùnliú' érxià

to flow downstream

25. 峡 xiá（名）

gorge

26. 陡 dǒu（形）

steep

27. 江面 jiāngmiàn（名）

the surface of a river

28. 窄 zhǎi（形）

narrow

29. 曲折 qūzhé（形）

winding

30. 撞 zhuàng（动）

to run into

31. 拐弯儿 guǎiwānr（动宾）

to turn a corner

○ 汽车要拐弯儿了，请大家坐好。

The car is going to make a turn. Please stay in your seat.

○ 再拐一个弯儿，我们就到博物馆了。

There is only one more turn before we get to the museum.

32. 诗 shī（名）

poem

诗人 shīrén（名）

poet

33. 两岸猿声啼不住 liǎng' àn yuánshēng tíbúzhù

Yet monkeys are still calling on banks behind me,

轻舟已过万重山 qīngzhōu yǐ guò wàn chóng shān

46

To my boat these ten thousand mountains away.

34. 港口 gǎngkǒu（名）

    port, harbour

35. 旅馆 lǚguǎn（名）

    hotel

36. 一天到晚 yītiāndàowǎn

    from morning to night

    ○ 上海的南京路一天到晚都很热闹。

    The Nanjing Road in Shanghai is busy all day from morning till night.

    ○ 一天到晚忙着学习，没机会出去游览。

    to be busy studying from morning to night without any chance to go sightseeing

37. 热闹 rènao（形）

    lively

38. 园林之城 yuánlín zhī chéng

    a city of gardens

39. 小巧 xiǎoqiǎo（形）

    small and exquisite

40. 别致 biézhì（形）

    uniquely elegant

41. 各 gè（代、副）

    each, every

    ○ 各民族文化都有自己的特色。

    The culture of every nationality has its own characteristics.

    ○ 参加的老师各写一封信。

    The participating teachers each wrote a letter.

42. 按照 ànzhào（介）

    according to

43. 建造 jiànzào（动）

    to build

44. 另外 lìngwài（代、副）

    in addition, moreover

    ○ 我说的是另外一回事。

    I am talking about something else.

    ○ 你们几个坐车走，另外的人坐船走。

You take the train and the others will go by boat.

○ 今天我有事，我们另外找时间谈吧。

I am tied up today. Let's have a talk some other time.

○ 另外，我们还游览了长城。

In addition，we also visited the Great Wall.

45. 三面环山 sān miàn huán shān

with mountains on three sides

46. 秀丽 xiùlì（形）

beautiful，pretty

47. 把……比作…… bǎ…bǐzuò…

to liken to

48. 女子 nǚzǐ（名）

woman

49. 民间 mínjiān（名）

folk

50. 传说 chuánshuō（名）

legend，folklore

51. 盒 hé（名）

box

52. 品尝 pǐncháng（动）

to taste

53. 亲眼 qīnyǎn（副）

to see with one's own eyes

○ 亲手

with one's own hands

○ 亲笔

in one's own handwriting

○ 亲口

say something personally

54. 进一步 jìnyībù（副）

further；to go a step further

○ 希望你进一步提高汉语水平。

I hope that you would further improve your Chinese.

○ 我们还不十分清楚，请你再进一步介绍一下好吗？

It is still not very clear to us；would you please explain it further?

55. 教导 jiàodǎo（名、动）
　　　teaching; to teach
56. 细（＋动）xì（＋V）（副）
　　　　　carefully; in detail
　　○ 细听
　　　to listen carefully
　　○ 细谈
　　　to talk about something in detail
57. 衷心 zhōngxīn（副）
　　　heartfelt
58. 祝 zhù（动）
　　　to wish, to express good wishes

专　名

1. 元	Yuán	the Yuan Dynasty
2. 明	Míng	the Ming Dynasty
3. 清	Qīng	the Qing Dynasty
4. 天安门广场	Tiān'ānmén Guǎngchǎng	Tian'anmen Square
5. 故宫	Gùgōng	the Palace Museum
6. 西安	Xī'ān	Xi'an
7. 秦	Qín	the Qin Dynasty
8. 汉	Hàn	the Han Dynasty
9. 唐	Táng	the Tang Dynasty
10. 秦始皇兵马俑 博物馆	Qín Shǐhuáng Bīngmǎyǒng Bówùguǎn	Museum of Emperor Qin Shihuang's Terra Cotta Cavalry
11. 重庆	Chóngqìng	Chongqing
12. 三峡	Sānxiá	the Three Gorges of the Yangtze River
13. 武汉	Wǔhàn	Wuhan
14. 纽约市	Niǔyuēshì	New York City
15. 西湖/西子湖	Xīhú/Xīzǐhú	the West Lake
16. 宋代	Sòng Dài	the Song Dynasty
17. 西施	Xīshī	Xishi, name of a patriotic beauty of the Spring and Autumn Period

49

18. 龙井茶　　　　　lóngjǐngchá　　　　*longjing*, a famous green tea produced in Hangzhou

语言点和练习

一、不但……而且……　not only... but also...

例句：

1. 琳达不但年轻，而且漂亮。

   Linda is not only young, but also pretty.

2. 他不但会英语，而且会汉语。

   He speaks not only English, but also Chinese.

3. 上海不但是中国最大的城市，而且也是中国最大的港口。

   Shanghai is not only the largest city, but also the largest seaport in China.

4. 杭州不但风景优美，而且名胜古迹很多。

   Hangzhou not only is beautiful, but also has many scenic spots and historical sites.

5. 不但我认识他，而且你也认识他。

   I am not the only person who knows him, you do too.

解释：

"不但……而且……"和"不只……而且……"一样，也表示除了所说的意思以外，还有进一层的意思。这种格式可以连接两个并列的词或短语，也可以连接两个并列的小句。

练习：

1. 用"不但……而且……"改写句子：

   (1) 他会作诗，也会画画儿。

   (2) 约翰喜欢打排球，也喜欢踢足球。

   (3) 我要学习中国地理，还要学习中国历史。

   (4) 苏州的园林小巧别致，各有特色。

   (5) 杭州很美，桂林也很美。

2. 完成句子：

(1) 那座山不但很高，_____。

(2) 长城不但在中国有名，_____。

(3) 北京_____，而且有很多有名的大学。

(4) 从重庆到上海_____，而且可坐飞机。

(5) 这篇文章不但内容丰富，_____。

(6) _____，而且长江和珠江也是从西往东流。

(7) _____，而且你也没见过他。

3. 用"不但……而且……"造句。

二、在……上 on, in

例句：

1. 他在工作上很努力。

   He works very hard at his job.

2. 北京、西安在历史上都相当重要。

   Both Beijing and Xǐan were very important in history.

3. 在生活上我要求不高。

   I prefer simplicity in my life.

4. 在学习上你要多帮助他。

   You should give him more help in his study.

解释：

"在……上"作状语，有时不表示具体的处所，而是表示在什么范围内，有"在……方面"的意思，可以在主语后边（例1、2），也可以在主语前边（例3、4）。

练习：

1. 用"在……上"填空：

(1) 上海_____占有重要的地位。

(2) 苏州_____很有特色。

(3) _____长城就很有名。

(4) 李老师 _____ 非
常认真。

(5) _____我们要互相帮助，_____我们要
互相关心。

2. 用"在……上"和所给的词语组成句子：

例：语言　　　特色

这本书在语言上很有特色。

(1)　　学习　　认真
(2)　　交通　　方便
(3)　　内容　　一样
(4)　　生活　　没有困难
(5)　　历史　　相当重要

三、好像　to seem, to be like

例句：

1. 我们好像见过面。

It seems that we have met before.

2. 好像他去过中国。

It seems that he has been to China.

3. 玛丽好像有点儿不舒服。

Mary looks like she is sick.

4. 到你这儿，好像到了自己家里一样。

I feel at home in your place.

5. 这个问题好像很简单，其实并不简单。

This question looks as if it were simple, but actually it is not.

解释：

"好像"有"仿佛、大概"的意思，表示不肯定的判断，如例1、2、
3，也有"类似、有些像"的意思，如例4、5、6。

练习：

1. 用下列词语组合句子：

(1) 他　汉语　学过　好像　三年
(2) 北京　好像　琳达　去过

(3) 屋子里　人　没有　好像

(4) 开演　电影　已经　好像　了

(5) 在　这儿　好像　小王　不

2. 用"好像"回答问题：

(1) A：这件衣服我穿着合适吗？

　　B：

(2) A：这两张画儿一样吗？

　　B：

(3) A：人们为什么把西湖比作漂亮的女子？

　　B：

(4) A：今天他为什么低着头，不说话？

　　B：

(5) A：那辆汽车是他的吗？

　　B：

四、各　each，every

例句：

1. 今天是星期日，各学校都不上课。

Today is Sunday. There is no school.

2. 他在这儿住过三年，各个方面的情况都很了解。

He used to live here for three years, so he knows everything.

3. 他们各作了一个句子。

They each made a sentence.

4. 这两本书在语言上各有特色。

As far as language is concerned, each of these two books has its own features.

5. 你们各看各的书，谁也不要说话。

Pay attention to your own reading. Nobody is allowed to talk.

解释：

"各＋（量）＋名"表示某个范围内所有的个体（如例1、2）。"各＋动"表示分别行动（如例3）或分别具有（如例4）。在强调分别作什么事、分别具有什么时，可以在宾语前加"各的"，成为"各＋动＋各的＋宾语"的格式（如例5）。"各有特色"也可以说成"各有各的特色"。

练习：

1. 把下列词组和句子译为英语：
   (1) 各位老师
   (2) 各位朋友
   (3) 各国的代表
   (4) 各学校的学生
   (5) 西安和上海各有特色。
   (6) 他们两个人各有各的缺点。
   (7) 请你用"了不起"和"连着"各作一个句子。
2. 用"各+动+各的"改写下列句子：
   例：小王正在看书，小李也正在看书。
   　　小王和小李正在各看各的书。
   (1) 苏州有苏州的特点，杭州有杭州的特点。
   (2) 咱们你做你的练习，我做我的练习吧。
   (3) 琳达回自己的宿舍了，玛丽也回自己的宿舍了。

五、之　of

例句：

1. 鱼米之乡　园林之城　旅客之家　千岛之国
   a land of fish and rice—a land of plenty; the city of gardens; a traveller's home; a country of a thousand islands
2. 风景之美　人数之多　内容之丰富　地位之重要
   the beauty of the scenery; the large number of people; the richness of content; the importance of a position (or status)

解释：

"之"，是古汉语保存下来的结构助词，用法大致相当于现代汉语的"的"。"之"可在修饰语和中心语（名词）之间（例1），也可在小句的主语和谓语之间，使这一小句变成名词性短语（例2）。

练习：

1. 把 (a) (b) (c) (d) 和 (1) (2) (3) (4) 搭配成句：

(1) 长江中下游	(a) 是旅客之家
(2) 苏州	(b) 是体育之窗
(3) 北京饭店	(c) 是鱼米之乡
(4) 下一个节目	(d) 是园林之城

2. 把 (a) (b) (c) (d) 和 (1) (2) (3) (4) 搭配成句:

(1) 杭州的风景之美	(a) 好像你写的一样
(2) 参加比赛的人数之多	(b) 跟西安差不多
(3) 这个城市历史地位之重要	(c) 是世界有名的
(4) 这篇文章语言之优美	(d) 我真没想到

六、按照　according to

例句:

1. 请大家按照课文的内容回答问题。

Please answer the questions according to the text.

2. 我们一定按照老师的教导认真学习。

We must study hard according to our teacher's instruction.

3. 我要按照大家的意见去做。

I will act according to your opinion.

4. 你应该按照大夫开的药方吃药。

You should take the medicine according to the doctor's prescription.

解释:

"按照"表示遵从某种标准,它所带的宾语一般多是双音节名词或以双音节名词为中心的短语。

练习:

1. 用"按照"和所给的词语回答问题:

(1) A: 这些练习怎么做?

　 B: ＿＿＿＿＿＿＿＿＿＿＿＿＿＿＿。(老师的要求)

(2) A: 今天的地理课老师是怎么讲的?

　 B: ＿＿＿＿＿＿＿＿＿＿＿＿＿＿＿。(地图)

(3) A: 这个问题怎么回答?

　 B: ＿＿＿＿＿＿＿＿＿＿＿＿＿＿＿。(课文内容)

(4) A: 汉字怎么才能写好呢?

B: _____。（我教的办法）

2．用"按照"和所给的词语造句：
(1)　按照　样子　建造
(2)　按照　方法　画画儿
(3)　按照　情况　去做
(4)　按照　要求　介绍

七、把……比作……　　to liken to

例句：

1．人们常把小孩儿比作花朵。

People usually liken children to flowers.

2．我们把年轻人比作早上的太阳。

We liken young people to the morning sun.

3．诗人把自己比作大海里的一滴水。

The poet likens himself to a drop of water in the ocean.

解释：

"把 A 比作 B"，是说 A 和 B 有相似之处，A 是要描写形容的人或物，也就是被比喻的对象，B 是用来比喻的人或物。一般地说，B 应该是具体的、形象的、生动的，为人们所熟悉的。

练习：

1．用"把……比作……"改写下列句子：
(1) 他说大海就像他的母亲。
(2) 诗人说自己好像一只小鸟。
(3) 那个话剧用梅花（plum）来比喻一位姑娘。
(4) 他们用松柏（pine）比喻两国人民的友谊（friendship）.

2．用"把……比作……"造句。

八、对……表示……　　to express. . . to

例句：

1．我们对各位朋友表示欢迎。

We express welcome to all our friends.

2. 我对你的进步（jìnbù）表示高兴。

I am very happy for your progress.

3. 大家都对你的健康表示关心。

Everybody is concerned about your health.

4. 对我的意见，他表示同意。

He expressed his consent to my opinion.

解释：

"对……表示……"是说用言语、行动对某人或某事表明某种态度。句子的主语可在"对……"前边（例1、2、3），也可在"对……"后边（例4），"表示"后边的宾语一般是表示感情意愿的双音节动词、形容词，如"欢迎""感谢""同意""高兴""满意"等，或者是双音节名词，如"意见""看法""态度"等。

练习：

1. 用"对……表示……"和所给的词组合句子：

　　（1）　旅行　满意

　　（2）　帮助　感谢

　　（3）　见面　高兴

　　（4）　访问　欢迎

　　（5）　学习　关心

2. 用"对……表示……"改写下列句子：

　　（1）大家都同意这个办法。

　　（2）我们欢迎各国朋友到北京大学来学习。

　　（3）这次游览西湖我们很高兴。

　　（4）我衷心感谢你对我的帮助。

听力练习

（听录音，听力问题见本书附录）

1. 请你简单地介绍一下北京的情况。
2. 西安有些什么名胜古迹？它在历史上有什么重要地位？
3. 请你说一说长江三峡有什么特色？
4. 为什么大多数到中国去的旅行团都到苏州杭州去游览？
5. 你的国家最有名的风景区在哪儿？请你介绍一下它的特色。
6. 请你介绍一下你参观过的博物馆。
7. 上海为什么是中国东南沿海最大的港口？
8. 你的国家的首都在哪儿？它在什么方面占重要的地位？
9. 请你说一件暑假发生的有意思的事情。
10. 请你介绍一下你的国家有名的园林的特色。
11. 说一个历史上有名的漂亮女子的故事。
12. 你有机会到外国去游览的时候，要到什么地方去？为什么？
13. 你学过中国诗没有？你最喜欢的诗人是谁？
14. 请你简单地说一说第一到第三课的内容对你进一步了解中国有什么帮助。
15. 这三课对中国的介绍你觉得最有意思的是什么？

翻译练习

(英译汉，答案见本书附录)

1. life during summer vacation
2. during summer vacation
3. to join a tour group
4. the places the tour group visited
5. to vist historical sites
6. to feel ill; to feel uncomfortable
7. to think it is important
8. the situation in agriculture
9. the architecture of the Tang Dynasty

10. the capital of the Han Dynasty

11. the magnificent Great Wall (of Ten Thousand Li)

12. wonderful buildings

13. special features of ancient places

14. 221 B.C.

15. at the beginning of the 21st century

16. quite magnificent

17. to hold an important position in the economy

18. status higher than others

19. not only interesting but also very important

20. the scenery of the Yangtze Gorges

21. the people on both sides of the straits

22. The mountain road is not only steep, it is also narrow.

23. following a narrow path

24. a complicated story

25. a famous poet

26. a port with highly developed industry and commerce

27. the hotels in the capital

28. busy working from morning till night

29. a lively square

30. Each had his own opinion.

31. according to the situation of each country

32. also visited the Palace Museum

33. to further raise the interest in research

34. to thank everyone for his help

35. to wish everyone good health

36. Chongqing is not only economically important but also culturally important.

37. The weather is so warm today that it seems as if it were already spring.

38. The first time I had American food was on the plane going to the States.

39. The ancient architecture of each country has its own characteristics.

40. Do you know which of the cities in the world is also called "the City of Music"?

41. Although we did it according to his idea, he is still unhappy.

42. Many students go to China to teach English and to study Chinese at the same time.

43. After careful consideration, I feel it is still more appropriate to do it this way.

44. The poem on this painting was put there by a famous ancient poet himself.

45. Children show interest in all things.

46. That foreign student expressed an interest in studying the position Xi'an held in history.

47. The content of this lesson is very important; we must read it carefully.

48. Each Chinese nationality has a fair amount of folktales from ancient times.

49. While we were in China we had to speak Chinese from morning till night.

50. When I relax, I like to listen to music and at the same time to savor good tea.

第 4 课

从炎黄子孙谈起

从炎黄子孙谈起

大家都知道，中国是一个历史悠久的国家。要讲中国历史，还要从中国人的祖先谈起。你们知道为什么中国人说自己是"黄帝子孙"，或者"炎黄子孙"吗？

传说黄帝是中国西北部一个部落的领袖。他跟炎帝的部落和其他部落联合在一起，在土地肥沃的黄河流域定居下来，形成了中华民族。

黄帝以后又出现了三个有名的领袖：尧、舜、禹。尧老了，把政权给了舜；舜老了，又把政权给了禹。你们听说过"大禹治水"的故事吗？传说尧、舜的时候，黄河年年发生水灾。禹带着很多人治水，走过了很多地方，几次经过自己家门口都没有进去看看。这样，经过了十三年，才把水治好了。

公元前二十一世纪，禹建立了中国第一个朝代——夏朝。关于夏朝的历史，我们知道的还不太多。公元前十七世纪，夏朝被商部落灭掉，开始了商朝。

商朝的文字是现在可以看到的中国最古的文字。从商朝的青铜器可以看出，当时的生产技术已经很高了。商朝最后一个统治者特别残暴，全国各地的人都起来反对他。公元前十一世纪，商朝灭亡了，周朝建立了。

周朝为了巩固政权，把土地分给一些贵族去统治，这些贵族就叫作诸侯。周朝的前二百多年，国都在现在的西安，历史上叫西周。公元前770年，周朝把国都迁到现在的洛阳，这以后就叫东周。为什么要把国都迁到洛阳去呢？有这样一个故事。

周幽王的妻子长得很美，可是特别不爱笑。有一天，幽王为了让她笑一笑，就想了一个办法，叫人到城外去点起烽火。诸侯看见烽火，以为敌人来了，就都立刻带兵跑来。幽王的妻子看见，果然笑了。不久，敌人真的来了。诸侯看见烽火，谁也不肯再来。结果，敌人杀了幽王，国都也被破坏了。幽王的儿子只好把国都迁到了东边的洛阳。

到了东周时期，周朝的统治一天比一天弱，诸侯国的势力一天比一天大，他们互相争权夺利，这就是历史上的春秋时期。后来，小国一个个被灭掉，只剩下七个大国，年年打仗，这就是战国时期。

春秋战国时期，社会发生了极大的变化，经济和文化都有很大的发展。那时候，人们的思想非常活跃，出现了很多有名的思想家、政治家、军事家和文学家。孔子是春秋时候的人，他的哲学思想和教育思想在中国产生了很大的影响。

秦始皇灭了六国，在公元前 221 年统一了中国，建立了中国历史上第一个中央集权的国家，这就是秦朝。秦朝对促进中国经济、文化的发展起了很大的作用。那时候，中国的势力就已经达到了现在的西南地区、东南沿海和珠江流域。秦始皇统一中国以后，把过去各诸侯国修的长城全部连起来，这就是世界有名的万里长城。

在秦朝统治下，人民生活很苦。秦始皇死后，他儿子做了皇帝，人民更活不下去了。他们觉得与其饿死，不如起来造反。于是，中国历史上第一次农民起义爆发了，秦朝不久就灭亡了。

1. **子孙** zǐsūn （名）
   descendents

2. **部落** bùluò （名）
   tribe

3. **领袖** lǐngxiù （名）
   leader，chieftain

4. **联合** liánhé （动）

   to unite

   ○ 联合国，妇女联合会，学生联合会
   the United Nations，Women's Federation，Student Union

5. **定居** dìngjū （动）

   to settle down，to reside permanently

   ○ 在中国定居的外国人大多数住在北京。
   Most of the foreign permanent residents in China live in Beijing.

6. **形成** xíngchéng （动）

   to form

   ○ 从很早以来，中国就形成了一个多民族的国家。
   For a long period of time China has been a multinational state.

   ○ 中国西部的高原和山脉是怎么形成的？
   How were the plateaus and mountains in the Western part of China formed?

7. **政权** zhèngquán （名）
   political power，regime

8. **建立** jiànlì （动）
   to establish

9. **关于** guānyú （介）
   about，concerning

10. **被** bèi （介）
    indicator of the passive voice

11. **灭掉** mièdiào （动补）
    to eliminate

12. **文字** wénzì（名）

   written language

13. **当时** dāngshí（名）

   at that time

14. **统治者** tǒngzhìzhě（名）

   ruler

   统治 tǒngzhì（动）

   to rule

   ……者 …zhě（尾）

   agent of an action; -er

   ○ 科学工作者，教育工作者

   scientific worker, educational worker

15. **残暴** cánbào（形）

   cruel, ruthless

16. **灭亡** mièwáng（动）

   to be destroyed

17. **巩固** gǒnggù（动、形）

   to consolidate; solid, stable

   ○ 只有经常复习，才能巩固学过的东西。

   Only if one reviews frequently, can one consolidate what one has learned.

   ○ 我以前学过两年汉语，但是学得不太巩固。

   I have previously studied Chinese for two years but what I have learned is not solid enough.

18. **分给** fēngěi（动补）

   to distribute

   分 fēn（动）

   to divide

   ○ 我从中国带回来几盒龙井茶，分给大家品尝品尝。

   I have brought back from China several boxes of *longjing* tea for everyone to enjoy.

   ○ 我们按照中文水平分三个班上课，我分到第一班。

   We have been divided into three classes according to our Chinese level and I have been put in the first class.

19. **贵族** guìzú（名）

noble; nobility, aristocrat

20. 诸侯 zhūhóu（名）

　　vassal

21. 搬 bān（动）

　　to move

○ 他家搬到上海去了。

　　His family had moved to Shanghai.

○ 请把这张桌子搬到那边去，你搬得动吗?

　　Please move this table over there. Can you manage?

○ 他搬来两把椅子，搬走一张桌子。

　　He brought two chairs and took away a table.

22. 妻子 qīzi（名）

　　wife

23. 点（起） diǎn（qǐ）（动）

　　　　to light

○ 点起火来

　　to light the fire

○ 点起灯来

　　to light the lamp

24. 烽火 fēnghuǒ（名）

　　beacon-fire

　火 huǒ（名）

　　fire

25. 以为 yǐwéi（动）

　　to think, to believe

○ 我以前以为黄河是中国最长的河，现在知道长江比黄河还长。

　　I used to think the Yellow River was the longest in China but now I know that the Yangtze River is even longer than the Yellow River.

○ 我以为要学好一门外语，一定要多听、多说。你以为怎么样?

　　I believe that in order to master a foreign language, one must speak and listen to the language as much as possible. What do you think of it?

26. 敌人 dírén（名）

　　enemy

27. 兵 bīng（名）

　　soldier

28. 果然 guǒrán（副）

　　sure enough

29. 杀 shā（动）

　　to kill

30. 破坏 pòhuài（动）

　　to destroy, to damage

31. 只好 zhǐhǎo（副）

　　to be forced to, to have to

32. 时期 shíqī（名）

　　period

33. 弱 ruò（形）

　　weak

34. 势力 shìlì（名）

　　force, power

35. 互相 hùxiāng（副）

　　mutual; each other

　　○ 同学们应该互相帮助、互相学习。

　　Students should help each other and learn from each other.

　　○ 让我们互相介绍一下。

　　Let us introduce ourselves.

36. 争权夺利 zhēngquánduólì

　　scramble for power and profit

37. 剩下 shèngxia（动补）

　　to be left

　　○ 下课后，大家都出去了，教室里只剩下我一个人。

　　After class everyone went out and I was the only one left in the class-room.

38. 打仗 dǎzhàng（动宾）

　　to fight a battle

39. 活跃 huóyuè（形）

　　active, lively

　　○ 她能唱歌，会跳舞，是我们班上最活跃的学生。

　　She can sing and dance, she is the liveliest student in our class.

　　○ 他讲话以后，会上的空气立刻活跃起来了。

　　After he gave his speech, the atmosphere of the meeting immediately became lively.

40. 哲学 zhéxué（名）

philosophy

41. 产生 chǎnshēng（动）

to come into being, to produce

○中国古代的文化是在黄河流域产生和发展起来的。

Ancient Chinese culture emerged and developed along the Yellow River
valley.

○新的教育方法产生了很好的效果（xiàoguǒ）。

The new pedagogical method yielded very good results.

42. 统一 tǒngyī（动、形）

to unify; uniform

○统一祖国

to reunite one's motherland

统一思想

to reach a common understanding

○思想统一

to have an integrated ideology

意见不统一

to have conflicting opinions

○统一的计划

a uniform plan

统一的意见

a unanimous opinion

43. 中央 zhōngyāng（名）

center

44. 集权 jíquán（动宾）

concentration of political power

45. 促进 cùjìn（动）

to promote

○我们用黄河的水发电、灌溉，促进了农业的发展。

We advanced the development in agriculture by making use of the Yellow
River to irrigate and to generate electricity.

○大家经常在一起谈谈，促进了互相的了解。

We often get together and talk, which has increased our mutual understanding.

○ 经济和文化可以互相促进。

Economy and culture can stimulate each other.

46. 达到 dádào（动）

to reach

○ 他的文化程度已经达到了大学的水平。

His education has reached college level.

○ 秦朝的影响达到了很远的地方。

The influence of the Qin Dynasty reached many far away places.

47. 修 xiū（动）

to fix，to repair

48. 皇帝 huángdì（名）

emperor

49. 与其……不如…… yǔqí…bùrú…

it's better... than

50. 造反 zàofǎn（动宾）

to rebel

51. 于是 yúshì（连）

therefore

52. 起义 qǐyì（名、动）

uprising；to revolt

53. 爆发 bàofā（动）

to break out

专 名

1. 黄帝	Huángdì	the Yellow Emperor
2. 炎帝	Yándì	Emperor Yan
3. 中华民族	Zhōnghuá Mínzú	the Chinese nation
4. 尧	Yáo	Yao
5. 舜	Shùn	Shun
6. 禹	Yǔ	Yu
7. 夏朝	Xià Cháo	the Xia Dynasty
8. 商朝	Shāng Cháo	the Shang Dynasty
9. 周朝	Zhōu Cháo	the Zhou Dynasty

东周	Dōng Zhōu	the Eastern Zhou Dynasty
西周	Xī Zhōu	the Western Zhou Dynasty
10. 洛阳	Luòyáng	Luoyang
11. 周幽王	Zhōu Yōuwáng	King You of Zhou Dynasty
12. 春秋	Chūnqiū	the Spring and Autumn Period
13. 战国	Zhànguó	the Warring States Period
14. 孔子	Kǒngzǐ	Confucius
15. 秦始皇	Qín Shǐhuáng	the First Emperor of the Qin Dynasty

语言点和练习

一、关于　concerning; about

例句：

1. 关于中国历史，我了解得很少。

   I know very little about Chinese history.

2. 关于西湖，有许多美丽的传说。

   There are many beautiful stories about the West Lake.

3. 关于怎样发展生产，他提出了很好的意见。

   He offered a very good proposal concerning how to develop production.

4. 我最喜欢看关于中国农村生活的电影。

   The movies that I like the best are those about the rural life in China.

5. 他给我们讲了一个关于大禹治水的故事。

   He told us a story about how Da Yu controlled floods.

解释：

"关于＋名词或动词/小句"表示牵涉到的事物。作状语时，"关于……"要放在主语前，一般用","号隔开。作定语时，在中心词前要加"的"。"对于……"是指明对象的，只能作状语，用在主语前后都可以。

练习：

1. 用"关于"或者"对于"填空：

70

(1) 我＿＿＿＿＿＿＿＿＿＿＿＿＿＿＿＿中国的民间故事很感兴趣。

(2) ＿＿＿＿＿＿黄帝怎样造创了中国古代的文化，有很多有意思的传说。

(3) 我最喜欢听＿＿＿＿＿＿＿＿＿＿＿中国古代历史的故事。

2．完成句子：

(1) 关于美国的地理环境，＿＿＿＿＿＿＿＿＿＿＿＿＿＿＿＿＿。

(2) 我最爱看关于＿＿＿＿＿＿＿＿＿＿＿＿＿＿＿＿电影。

(3) 关于周朝为什么把国都迁到东边去，＿＿＿＿＿＿＿。

3．用"关于"完成句子：

(1) ＿＿＿＿＿＿＿＿＿＿＿＿＿＿＿，他看了不少的书。

(2) 这是一篇＿＿＿＿＿＿＿＿＿＿＿＿＿＿＿文章。

(3) 你喜欢不喜欢看＿＿＿＿＿＿＿＿＿＿＿＿＿＿画报？

(4) ＿＿＿＿＿＿＿＿＿＿＿＿＿＿＿，你有什么意见？

二、被 indicator of the passive voice

例句：

1．他在路上被自行车撞了一下。

He was struck by a bicycle in the street.

2．我的字典被小王借走了。

My dictionary was borrowed by Xiao Wang.

3．那个工厂被敌人破坏了。

That factory was destroyed by the enemies.

4．那个残暴的统治者被人民杀死了。

That cruel and ferocious ruler was killed by the people.

5．那个工厂被（人）破坏了。

That factory was destroyed.

6．那个残暴的统治者被（人）杀死了。

That cruel and ferocious ruler was killed.

解释：

"被"用于被动句引进施动者，前面的主语是动作的受动者。"被"字句的动词后面一般要有表示完成或者结果的成分，如结果补语、趋向补语、动量补语、"了"等等。"被"后面的施动者如果是不言而喻的，可以用"被人"，甚至连"人"也省去。

"被"字句的词序是："受动者＋被（＋施动者）＋动词＋其他成分"。要注意的是如果主语和动词只能是受动关系，不会使人误解为施动关系，在施动者不出现时，动词前不要加"被"字。（如"这本书已经看完了。"）

练习：

1. 以下空白里，在必要的地方填"被"，说出哪些地方不用"被"，以及不能用"被"的原因：

(1) 敌人＿＿＿＿＿＿我们打跑了。

(2) 那本字典＿＿＿＿＿＿买到了没有？

(3) 我的自行车已经＿＿＿＿＿＿修理好了。

(4) 二百多年以前，那个城市＿＿＿＿＿＿敌人破坏了。

(5) 商朝最后一个统治者是个非常残暴的人，他最后＿＿＿＿＿＿杀了。

(6) 长城是什么时候＿＿＿＿＿＿修的？

(7) 那几个小国都＿＿＿＿＿＿秦国灭了。

(8) 商朝的文字现在还可以＿＿＿＿＿＿看到吗？

2. 把下面的句子改成"被"字句：

(1) 商部落灭了夏朝。

(2) 敌人破坏了周朝的国都。

(3) 汽车把他撞死了。

(4) 敌人把那些古建筑破坏了。

三、为了　for the sake of；in order to

例句：

1. 为了进一步了解中国，我想到中国去亲眼看看是什么样子。

   In order to have a better understanding of China, I would like to go to China and see by myself what is happening there.

2. 为了发展工业，我们必须增加煤和石油的生产。

   For the sake of developing industry, we have to increase the production of coal and petroleum.

3. 这些青年为了提高文化水平，正在努力学习。

   In order to raise their educational level these young people are studying hard.

4. 为了身体健康，我们要经常锻炼。

In order to keep fit，we have to exercise regularly.

解释：

"为了……"作状语表示目的，可以用在主语前面或后面。

练习：

1. 用"为了"把下面表示目的和手段的短语连成句子（可以加词，短语可以拆开。）

           目的   手段

   (1) 治好大水、走过自己的家没有进去

   (2) 学好汉语、互相帮助

   (3) 了解中国历史、参观中国历史博物馆

   (4) 坐早上七点钟的火车、五点半就起床

   (5) 锻炼身体、经常游泳

   (6) 欢迎新同学、开联欢会

2. 用"为了"改句子：

   (1) 琳达给老师写了一封信，告诉老师她在中国游览的经过。

   (2) 我给他写了一封信，表示感谢他对我的帮助。

   (3) 我们住在离海岸不远的一个旅馆里，这样可以每天去游泳。

   (4) 今年暑假我没回家，因为在学校里可以多念一点书。

四、前 + ［数］+ ［量］(+ ［名］)　　first + NU + M (+ N)

例句：

1. 练习里前两个问题特别难。

   The first two questions in the exercise are most difficult.

2. 前十课（课文）都很容易，没有太多的生词。

   The first ten lessons are very easy because they do not have too many new words.

3. 我在大学学习了四年，前两年我学的是历史，后两年学的是文学。

   I went to college for four years. I studied history in the first two years, and literature in the last two.

4. 刚开学的前两个月他病了，没来上课。

He was sick in the first two months of the school, so he did not come to class.

解释:

"前"（或"后"）和数量短语结合，表示按顺序或时间在前面（或"后面"）的那一部分。

练习:

1. 用"前＋［数］＋［量］＋（［名］)"回答问题:

(1) 这些生词你都学过吗？

(2) 这几课课文你都看得懂吗？

(3) 那几个问题他回答得怎么样？

(4) 去年你一年都在北京吗？

(5) 那些人正由西往东走呢！你认识他们吗？

(6) 上星期你来上课了吗？

五、果然　sure enough; as expected

例句:

1. 大家都说这个电影好。看了以后，我觉得果然不错。

Everyone said this is a good movie. After I went to see it, I really thought so.

2. 常常练习听、说，他的中文水平果然提高了。

Having frequently practiced listening and speaking, his Chinese has improved as expected.

3. 到了大草原一看，果然是"天苍苍，野茫茫，风吹草低见牛羊"。

Upon arriving at the grasslands, it was true that "blue, blue the sky; vast, vast the fields; the grasses are blown; the cattle are shown".

解释:

"果然"表示发现事实或结果和所说的或预料的一样。用在谓语动词或形容词前。有时也用在主语前。

练习:

1. 用"果然"完成句子:

74

(1) 中国人常说："上有天堂，下有苏杭"，＿＿＿＿＿＿＿＿＿＿。

(2) 看了地图，我知道＿＿＿＿＿＿＿＿＿＿＿＿＿＿＿。

(3) 登上长城一看，＿＿＿＿＿＿＿＿＿＿＿＿＿＿。

(4) 纽约的"明轩"＿＿＿＿＿＿＿＿＿＿＿＿＿＿。

(5) 北京可游览的名胜古迹＿＿＿＿＿＿＿＿＿＿＿。

2. 用"果然"和下面的短语造句：

(1) 非常热闹　　　(2) 生产提高

(3) 风景秀丽　　　(5) 特别发达

(4) 进步得很快　　(6) 产生……影响

六、结果　as a result

例句：

1. 你们的讨论有没有结果？讨论的结果怎么样？

Have you come to any conclusion? What was the result of your discussion?

2. 全国的人都起来反对商朝，结果商朝灭亡了。

People all over the country stood up to rebel; as a result, the Shang Dynasty was destroyed.

3. 在秦朝统治下，人民生活很苦，结果爆发了农民起义。

Under the rule of the Qin Dynasty, people had a miserable life; as a result, the peasant uprising broke out.

4. 大家都努力生产，结果产品增加了一倍。

Everyone is working very hard; as a result, the output has been doubled.

解释：

"结果"本来是名词。作为连词"结果"连接两个分句，表示由于前面那件事或那种情况，产生了后面的结果。

练习：

1. 用"结果"和下面的词、短语连成句子：

(1) 他不小心、摔下来

(2) 努力学习新技术、生产水平、进一步、提高

(3) 经过讨论、意见、统一

(4) 下大雨、雨水太多、生产、受……影响

2. 用"结果"完成句子：
   (1) 我们想去参观一个博物馆，可是后来下雨了，＿＿＿＿＿＿＿。
   (2) 黄帝的部落和炎帝的部落联合在一起，＿＿＿＿＿＿＿。
   (3) 他每天早上跑步，锻炼身体，＿＿＿＿＿＿＿。
   (4) 这条河从上游带下来大量泥沙，＿＿＿＿＿＿＿。

七、只好　to have to；to be forced to

例句：

1. 我不懂英语，只好请他翻译。
   I do not know English and I have to ask him to translate for me.
2. 那里耕地不多，人们只好靠放牧生活。
   The cultivated area there is very limited, so people have to live on pasturing.
3. 他们都不肯去，只好我一个人去了。
   None of them is willing to go, so I have to go by myself.

解释：
"只好"表示没有别的办法，"不得不……"。一般用在谓语动词的前面。有时也用在主语的前面。如例3。

练习：

1. 用"只好"完成句子：
   (1) 这里的交通不太方便，不但没有飞机，而且没有火车，
       ＿＿＿＿＿＿＿＿＿＿＿＿＿＿＿＿。
   (2) 我不会用中文写信，＿＿＿＿＿＿＿＿＿＿＿＿。
   (3) 他的右手坏了，＿＿＿＿＿＿＿＿＿＿＿＿。
   (4) 在秦朝统治下，农民生活不下去，＿＿＿＿＿＿＿＿。
   (5) 那个地方气候太冷，而水又很少，不能种水稻，＿＿＿＿＿。
2. 用"只好"回答问题：
   (1) 你为什么一个人来？
   (2) 你们为什么不去看电影？
   (3) 你不是有钢笔吗？为什么又买了一枝？
   (4) 今年暑假你为什么不回家？

76

八、一天比一天　day by day

例句:

1. 现在是十一月，天气一天比一天冷了。

   It is now November, and it's getting colder day by day.

2. 人民的生活一天比一天好。

   People's lives are getting better and better every day.

3. 这个港口的工商业一天比一天发达。

   The industry and commerce at this port are developing daily.

解释:

"一天比一天＋形容词"表示程度不断加深。

练习:

1. 用"一天比一天"和下面的词和短语连成句子:

   (1) 六月、热　　　　　　(5) 兴趣、大

   (2) 经济地位、重要　　　(6) 身体、好

   (3) 生产技术、高　　　　(7) 人口、多

   (4) 交通、方便

2. 用"一天比一天"回答问题:

   (1) 那里农民的生活怎么样?

   (2) 春天到了，天气不那么冷了吧?

   (3) 他的健康情况怎么样?

   (4) 那里生产的石油多不多?

九、一个个（地、的）　one by one

例句:

1. 人们一个个地从汽车上走下来。

   One by one people got off the bus.

2. 他正在一个个地查这些生词。

   He is looking them up in the dictionary word by word.

3. 校园里的新楼一座座地修建起来了。

   One after another, new buildings have been built on the campus.

4．那里一座座的宫殿都非常雄伟壮观。

Every one of the palaces there is imposing and magnificent.

5．墙上挂满了一张张的画片。

Pictures are hanging all over the wall.

解释：

"一＋量词重叠（＋地)"作状语表示多而按先后次序进行。

"一＋量词重叠＋的"作定语，形容多而又整齐。"一＋量词重叠"又作"一＋量＋一＋量"。(如："一座一座地修建起来了"，"一座一座的宫殿")

练习：

1．在适当的地方加上"一＋量词重叠＋地"：

例：房子都修好了。→房子一座座地都修好了。

(1) 困难问题都解决了。

(2) 那些发电站都建立起来了。

(3) 节目表演完了。

(4) 那么多水果他都吃完了。

(5) 为了找那篇文章，这些杂志我都看过了。

2．在适当的地方加上"一＋量词重叠＋的"（必要时可以减去一些字）：

例：书架上摆着很多新书。→书架上摆着一本本的新书。

(1) 那里的新房子修得真漂亮。

(2) 他们走过了很多高山。

(3) 桌子上放着很多画报和杂杂。

(4) 很多辆汽车开过去了。

(5) 我们登上长城，看见四周都是山峰。

十、与其……不如……　better... than...

例句：

1．我们与其跑出去看电影，不如在家看电视。

It is better for us to stay at home watching television than to go out for a movie.

2．从重庆到武汉，与其坐飞机，不如坐船。

To go from Chongqing to Wuhan, it is better to go by boat than by plane.

3. 你与其靠别人帮助，不如靠自己努力。

It is better for you to try by yourself than to rely upon others.

解释：

"与其 A 不如 B"连接两个短语或分句，表示比较 A 和 B 两种作法，说话人认为 B 的作法比 A 好。"不如"可以单用。"A 不如 B"就是"A 没有 B 好"，"B 比 A 好"。"A 不如 B（大）"就是"A 没有 B（大）"，也就是"B 比 A（大）"。例如："这间教室不如那间教室"意思是"这间教室没有那间教室好"。"这间教室不如那间教室大"意思是"这间教室没有那间教室大"。

练习：

1. 比较下面 A、B 两种作法，认为 B 的作法比 A 好。用"与其……不如……"来表示：

例：A. 坐火车 B. 坐汽车→与其坐火车不如坐汽车。

(1) A. 骑自行车   B. 走路

(2) A. 明天开始   B. 今天马上开始

(3) A. 分几个小组讨论   B. 集中在一起讨论

(4) A. 写得太长   B. 写得简单清楚一些

(5) A. 给他写信   B. 给他打电话

2. 用"与其……不如……"改句子：

(1) 我们去上海坐飞机比坐火车好。

(2) 你平常注意锻炼身体，比生了病再吃药好。

(3) 我们今天晚上把工作作完，比明天早上做好。

(4) 亲眼去看看那里的情况，比听别人介绍好。

3. 用"A 没有 B…"，再用"B 比 A…"改下面的句子：

(1) 这本书不如那本书。

(2) 这个公园不如那个公园大。

(3) 小王的英语不如小张。

(4) 他来得不如我早。

(5) 他觉得北方不如南方。

(6) 北方不如南方暖和。

十一、于是 *therefore*

例句:

1. 很久以前,中国人的祖先就在黄河流域生活、劳动,于是中国古代文化就从这里发展起来了。

   Long ago the ancestors of the Chinese people had been living and working along the Yellow River; thus it was there that the ancient Chinese culture developed.

2. 听说西安的名胜古迹很多,于是我们就坐火车去西安了。

   Having heard that there are many scenic spots and historical sites in Xi'an, we took a train there.

3. 那个地方矿产资源特别丰富,于是人们把那里建设成一个重要的能源基地。

   People have turned that place into an important base of energy resources because the mineral products are very rich there.

解释:

"于是"连接两个分句,表示后面的一件事是从前面的一件事自然引出的结果。

练习:

用"于是"完成句子:

1. 听说那个地方一年四季都像春天一样,＿＿＿＿＿＿＿＿。

2. 看完电影,时间还早,＿＿＿＿＿＿＿＿＿＿＿＿。

3. 我和一个朋友去书店买书,看见一种汉英字典。我朋友说,这种字典很好,对我学习中文很有帮助,＿＿＿＿＿＿＿＿＿＿。

4. 小王生病了,我去医院看他。路上遇见小张,他说也想去看小王,＿＿＿＿＿＿。

5. 舜觉得禹是个肯替人民作事情的人,可以作人民的领袖,＿＿＿＿＿＿＿＿＿＿＿＿＿。

（听录音，听力问题见本书附录）

回答问题

1. 请你谈一谈中华民族是怎么样形成的？
2. 为什么舜老了，不把政权交给别人，交给了禹？
3. 请介绍一下商朝的情况。
4. 周朝为什么要迁都？迁到了哪儿？
5. 请你详细地说一说东周时期君主跟诸侯的关系。
6. 战国时代为什么年年打仗？
7. 战国时代年年打仗产生什么样的结果，这对中国历史有什么影响？
8. 为什么春秋时代思想特别活跃？
9. 秦朝在中国历史上有什么重要作用？请你详细地说一说。
10. 请你说一说为什么秦朝那么快就灭亡了？

翻译练习

（英译汉，答案见本书附录）

1. to begin by talking about the ancestors
2. to unite the leaders of the tribes
3. the national minorities that had settled down in the North
4. to form a nation
5. to form the topography of a basin
6. often appeared along the coastal areas
7. about the legend of the West Lake
8. about the formation of the written language

9. was destroyed by another tribe
10. to raise the technical level
11. at that time the ruler that opposed the development of new technology
12. in order to consolidate the new established regime
13. to oppose the rule of the vassals
14. to move one's family to China
15. Sure enough, the enemy brought their soldiers.
16. In the end all were killed.
17. the regime that was weak
18. the weak countries that were destroyed
19. the Spring and Autumn Period and the Warring States Period
20. The ancient buildings were destroyed.
21. had to move the things away
22. influenced each other
23. (His) thinking has changed.
24. a city with a very active commerce
25. to study ancient Chinese philosophy
26. Great changes occured.
27. under the leadership of the central (government)
28. to promote unity
29. Its influence reached the Yangtze River valley.
30. the workers participating in the road construction
31. the emperors in Chinese history
32. It's better to go by boat than by train.
33. Nobody knows clearly how he was killed.
34. How is the culture of a multinational country formed?
35. The lives of the peasants have improved with each day.
36. In the end, they all got ill.
37. People of other nationalities also came here to live; therefore a multinational area was formed.
38. To promote the development of transportation many roads were built in that area.
39. I thought there would not be many participants at this party. Actually, many came.
40. The unification of the language has a great effect on promoting the unity of

the nationalities.

41. The scrambling for power and profit resulted in the elimination of the smaller states.

42. At that time, production techniques had reached quite a high level.

43. At the time when the emperor distributed the land to the vassals, their power was still weak.

44. Confucius was not only a philosopher, he was also an educator.

45. What effect did Emperor Qin Shibuang's unifying the written language have on the Chinese culture?

46. Did the establishment of the United Nations promote unity among the nations of the world?

47. During the Warring States Period, all schools of thought were very active.

48. When did China become a state with a centralized political power?

49. There were quite a lot of famous thinkers during the Spring and Autumn Period.

50. The remaining students moved out one by one.

第5课

"汉人"和"唐人"的由来

"汉人"和"唐人"的由来

老师：大家已经预习过了汉朝到唐朝的历史，还有哪些地方不太清楚，可以提出来讨论。

约翰：汉朝是什么时候建立的？

彼得：秦朝以后就是汉朝。汉朝建立在公元前202年，它一共经过四百多年，是个相当长的朝代。

玛丽：为什么说汉朝是中国历史上强盛的时期？是不是汉武帝的时候最强？

汤姆：汉朝刚建立的时候，北方的匈奴常常来侵扰。到了汉武帝，国家力量强大了，才派兵打败了匈奴。

琳达：汉武帝还发展了和中亚各国的友好往来，打通了去西域的路。

约翰：老师，西域是什么地方？

老师：那时候，人们把中国西部的新疆和中亚地区都叫做西域。

琳达：是啊！丝绸就是那时候介绍到西域的。西域的人特别喜欢中国的丝绸，所以人们就把汉朝和西域通商的这条路叫做"丝绸之路"。

玛丽：老师，关于"和亲"政策，您能举个例子来说明一下吗？

老师：啊！中国民间流传着一个王昭君的故事，我就给大家讲讲吧。汉武帝以后，又过了几十年，有个匈奴领袖愿意和汉朝友好，想娶一个汉朝的公主。王昭君原来是一个宫女，为了汉朝和匈奴的友好关系，就嫁到匈奴那里去了。

汤姆：《史记》是一部什么书？

老师：《史记》是司马迁写的。这部书记载了中国从黄帝到汉武帝三千年的历史，最主要的部分是人物传记。他写的各种人物都特别形象、生动。所以这部书既是伟大的历史著作，又是优秀的文学著作。

彼得：老师，三国时期是在汉朝吗？

老师：汉朝末年就是三国时期。以后中国有相当长的一段时间是分裂的，北方常常是少数民族统治，到公元589年隋朝才统一了中国。不过，隋朝非常短。它的第二个皇帝非常残暴。这时又爆发了农民起义，隋朝不久就灭亡了。

琳达：中国从南到北的大运河，不是隋朝时候修的吗？

老师：对。修运河虽然给当时的人民带来灾难，但是对南北交通起了很大的作用。

玛丽：隋朝以后是唐朝。现在还有人用"唐人"代表中国人，这可能和唐朝有关系吧？

约翰：当然了！因为唐朝是中国历史上特别强盛的时期嘛！正像"汉语""汉族"这些词是从汉朝来的一样。老师，对不对？

老师：说得很对。

彼得：唐太宗是个什么样的人？为什么唐太宗的时候中国经济特别繁荣？

汤姆：唐太宗是中国历史上一位杰出的政治家。他从隋朝很快灭亡这件事吸取了教训，认识到要巩固自己的政权，必须让人民过安定的生活。他还有一个很大的优点，就是能听别人的意见。

玛丽：老师，请您谈谈唐朝的文化好吗？

老师：好。唐朝时候，中国文化发展得很快，特别是诗歌达到了高峰。当时出现了很多杰出的诗人，像李白、杜甫等。他们写出了大量的优秀作品。那时候，日本、朝鲜等国家都派留学生来学习中国文化。唐朝的和尚玄奘也不远万里到印度去取经。

琳达：唐朝后来为什么衰落下去了呢？

老师：唐玄宗到了老年，整天和杨贵妃吃喝玩乐，不再关心国家大事，结果国家发生了一次大动乱。唐玄宗慌忙带着杨贵妃等人离开国都长安，想逃到四川去。但是在路上士兵们由于恨杨贵妃和她哥哥杨国忠，不肯前进。

他们杀了杨国忠，结果杨贵妃也被迫上吊死了。

玛丽：后来呢？

老师：唐玄宗逃到四川以后，他儿子做了皇帝。国家又经过了八年的战争，人民遭到很多的灾难，社会和经济遭到很大的破坏。从这以后，唐朝就衰落下去了。

生　词

1. **强盛** qiángshèng（形）

   （of a country）powerful and prosperous

2. **侵扰** qīnrǎo（动）

   to invade and harass

3. **力量** lìliang（名）

   power，strength

4. **强大** qiángdà（形）

   big and powerful

5. **派** pài（动）

   to send，to assign

   ○ 中国派很多留学生到国外去学习。

   Many Chinese students were sent to study abroad.

   ○ 他毕业以后被派到青藏高原去工作。

   After he graduated from the school he was assigned to work in the Qing-hai-Tibet Plateau.

6. **打败** dǎbài（动补）

   to defeat

7. **往来** wǎnglái（名、动）

   contact；to come and go

   ○ 中国发展了和世界各国人民的友好往来。

   China has developed friendly contacts with various people all over the world.

   ○ 他们几个好朋友经常往来。

   They are good friends and they see each other very often.

8. **打通** dǎtōng（动补）

   to get through，to open up

   通 tōng（形）

   to open；through

   ○ 前面正在修路，这条路不通。

   This road has been blocked because the road ahead is under construction.

   ○ 电话打通了。

The call has been put through.

9. 丝绸 sīchóu（名）

silk

10. 通商 tōngshāng（动宾）

(of nations) have trade relations

11. "和亲" 政策 "héqīn" zhèngcè

(of some feudal dynasties) a policy of appeasement by marry-
ing daughters of the Han imperial family to minority rulers

政策 zhèngcè（名）

policy

12. 例子 lìzi（名）

example

13. 说明 shuōmíng（动、名）

to explain, to illustrate; directions

○ 这个机器怎么用？请他来说明一下。

How does this machine operate? Please ask him to explain.

○ 农民起义推翻了秦朝的统治，说明人民的力量是很大的。

The Qin Dynasty was overthrown by the peasant uprising, which shows the
tremendous strength of the people.

○ 展览会上每个图片下面都有说明。

There is a caption beneath every picture displayed in the exhibition.

14. 流传 liúchuán（动）

to circulate, to hand down

○ 从古以来民间就流传着很多关于大禹治水的故事。

Since ancient times many stories about how Yu brought the floods under
control have been told among the people.

15. 娶 qǔ（动）

to marry（a woman）

16. 公主 gōngzhǔ（名）

princess

17. 原来 yuánlái（副、形、连）

originally; former

○ 他原来是个工人，现在在大学学习。

Formerly he was a worker, now he is studying in the college.

○ 我也觉得我原来的句子不太对。

I also think my original sentence is not quite right.

18. 宫女 gōngnǔ（名）

    a maid in an imperial palace

19. 嫁 jià（动）

    to marry（a man）

20. 关系 guānnxi（名）

    relation, relationship

    ○ 这两个国家最近建立了友好关系。

    These two countries have recently established friendly relations.

    ○ 那里适合种棉花，这一定和气候有关系吧。

    That area is suitable for growing cotton. It must have something to do with the weather.

21. 记载 jìzǎi（动、名）

    to record; records

    ○ 按照历史的记载，那件事发生在秦国统一六国以前。

    According to historical records, that event took place before the six states were unified by the State of Qin.

    ○《诗经》记载了当时人民的生活。

    The *Book of Odes* recorded the life of the people at that time.

22. 人物 rénwù（名）

    character, figure

23. 传记 zhuànjì（名）

    biography

24. 形象 xíngxiàng（名、形）

    image, form; vivid

    ○ 这本小说里的人物都写得非常形象。

    All the characters in this novel are vividly depicted.

    ○ 我特别喜欢这个电影里那个青年工人的形象。

    In this movie, I especially like the image of that young worker.

25. 生动 shēngdòng（形）

    vivid, lively

26. 部 bù（量）

    （measure word for books, machines, etc.）

    ○ 一部电影

    a film

○ 一部历史著作

a work of history

27. 既……又…… jì…yòu…

both... and, as well as

28. 优秀 yōuxiù（形）

excellent, outstanding

29. 著作 zhùzuò（名）

work, writings

30. 末年 mònián（名）

last years of a dynasty or a reign

31. 分裂 fēnliè（动）

to split, to divide

○ 1945 年以后德国被分裂成两个国家。

After 1945 Germany has been divided into two countries.

○ 我们不清楚产生分裂的原因。

We are not clear about the reason which caused the split.

32. 不过 bùguò（连）

yet, but, however

33. 运河 yùnhé（名）

canal

34. 灾难 zāinàn（名）

disaster, catastrophe

35. 代表 dàibiǎo（动、名）

to represent; delegate

○ 他代表全班同学在会上介绍了学习中文的经验。

During the conference, he gave a speech on behalf of his class describing the experience of learning Chinese.

○ 他被选为全国人民代表。

He has been elected to be the people's representative.

36. 繁荣 fánróng（形、动）

flourishing; to make something prosper

○ 经济繁荣

a booming economy

○ 繁荣经济

to bring about a prosperous economy

92

37. 杰出 jiéchū（形）

   prominent，remarkable

38. 吸取 xīqǔ（动）

   to absorb，to draw

39. 教训 jiàoxùn（名、动）

   lesson；to teach somebody a lesson

40. 认识到 rènshidào

      to realize

41. 安定 āndìng（形）

   stable，settled

42. 优点 yōudiǎn（名）

   merit，strong point

43. 作品 zuòpǐn（名）

   work（of literature and art）

44. 和尚 héshang（名）

   monk

45. 不远万里 bùyuǎnwànlǐ

      to go to the trouble of travelling a long distance

46. 取经 qǔjīng（动宾）

   to go on a pilgrimage for Buddhist scriptures；to learn from somebody
   else's experience

47. 衰落 shuāiluò（动）

   to decline

48. 整天 zhěngtiān（名）

   the whole day，all day long

49. 吃喝玩乐 chīhēwánlè

      to eat，drink and be merry—idle away one's time in pleasure-
      seeking

50. 动乱 dòngluàn（名）

   disturbance，upheaval

51. 慌忙 huāngmáng（形）

   in a great rush

52. 逃 táo（动）

   to flee，to escape

   ○ 敌人都逃走了。

All the enemies fled.

○ 由于水灾，那年他们全家逃到了这里。

Fleeing from the flood, his whole family came here that year.

53. 恨 hèn（动）

    to hate, to regret

54. 前进 qiánjìn（动）

    to go forward, to advance

55. 被迫 bèipò

    to be forced

○ 敌人被迫投降了。

The enemy were forced to surrender.

56. 上吊 shàngdiào（动）

    to hang by the neck, to hang oneself

57. 遭到 zāodào（动补）

    to suffer, to encounter

○ 遭到破坏

    to suffer damage

○ 遭到失败

    to meet with defeat

专　名

1. 汉武帝	Hàn Wǔdì	Emperor Wudi of the Han Dynasty
2. 匈奴	Xiōngnú	Huns（an ancient nationality in China）
3. 中亚	Zhōng Yà	Central Asia
4. 西域	Xīyù	the Western Regions（a Han Dynasty term for the area which is now Xinjiang and parts of Central Asia）
5. 王昭君	Wáng Zhāojun	Wang Zhaojun（a famous beauty in ancient time）
6. 史记	Shǐjì	*Records of the Historian*（by Sima Qian）
7. 司马迁	Sīmǎ Qiān	Sima Qian
8. 三国	Sānguó	the Three Kingdoms
9. 隋朝	Suí Cháo	the Sui Dynasty
10. 唐太宗	Táng Tàizōng	Emperor Taizong of the Tang Dynasty

11. 李白	Lǐ Bái	Li Bai（a famous poet in the Tang Dynasty）
12. 杜甫	Dù Fǔ	Du Fu（a famous poet in the Tang Dynasty）
13. 日本	Rìběn	Japan
14. 朝鲜	Cháoxiǎn	Korea
15. 玄奘	Xuánzàng	Xuanzang，a famous monk in the Tang Dynasty
16. 唐玄宗	Táng Xuánzōng	Emperor Xuanzong of the Tang Dynasty
17. 杨贵妃	Yáng Guìfēi	Lady Yang
18. 杨国忠	Yáng Guózhōng	Yang Guozhong（Lady Yang's brother）

语言点和练习

一、才   only then; not until

例句：

1. 昨天下午我们五点才下课。

   Yesterday afternoon we did not get out of class until 5 o'clock.

2. 他到三十岁才开始学外语。

   He did not begin to learn any foreign language until thirty years old.

3. 这句话的意思，老师讲过以后，我才懂了。

   After the teacher explained the meaning of the sentence, I understood it.

4. 看了她的信，我才知道她到中国去了。

   I did not know that she had gone to China until I read her letter.

5. 我还在学习，明年才能毕业。

   I am now still at school. I will not graduate until next year.

解释：

"才"表示动作发生或结束得晚。前面或者有表示时间晚的词语，或者有表示必不可少的条件或原因的短语或分句。除用于已完成的动作外，也能用于未完成的动作，如后两个例句跟"才"的意思和作用相反的是"就"。

练习：

1. 完成句子：

(1) _____，我才开始学中文。

(2) _____，我才休息。

(3) _____，他才回国。

(4) _____，这个旅行团才离开中国。

(5) 秦始皇_____，才把过去修的长城连接起来。

(6) 夏朝以后不是周朝，_____才是周朝。

(7) _____，汉朝才打败了匈奴。

(8) _____，这里才变成一个人口很多的大城市。

(9) _____，他才知道中国是一个多民族的国家。

2. 用"才"或者"就"完成句子：

(1) 我们坐上火车，只用一小时_____。

(2) 我细看了半天，_____。

(3) 我在上海只住了一夜，第二天早上_____。

(4) 邮局离这儿不远，一拐弯儿_____。

(5) 飞机场离这儿很远，坐汽车_____。

(6) 船在江上顺流而下，不到半天_____。

(7) 经过长时间的治理，_____。

(8) 我亲眼看见农民生活的情况，_____。

(9) 农民起义爆发了，秦朝不久_____。

二、（把）……叫做…… to call... as...

例句：

1. 这种花叫（做）什么花？

   What do you call this kind of flower?

2. 西湖又叫（做）"西子湖"。

   The West Lake is also called Xizi Lake.

3. 人们把历史上那个时期叫做春秋时期。

   That period in history is called the Spring and Autumn Period.

96

4. 有的地方把自行车叫做"单车"。

In some places a bicycle is called 单车.

解释：

"A 叫做 B"是"A 被称为 B"的意思。可以省为"A 叫 B"。如果用施动者作主语，往往用"主语—把—A 叫做 B"的句式。这时"叫做"一般不能省为"叫"。

练习：

用"叫做"或者"把……叫做……"连接句子：

1. 长城　　　　　　　万里长城
2. 苏州　　　　　　　园林之城
3. 商业最繁荣的地方　商业中心
4. 汉朝末年　　　　　三国时期
5. 中国人　　　　　　唐人
6. 这种花　　　　　　月季花（rose）

三、既……又…… both... and...

例句：

1. 他既是文学家又是哲学家。

He is both a man of letters and a philosopher.

2. 这座房子既有中国建筑的特色，又有现代的设备。

This house has both the features of Chinese architecture and modern facilities.

3. 那里既生产水稻，又生产小麦。

Both rice and wheat are grown there.

4. 这个地方气候特别好，既不太冷，又不太热。

The climate here is very good: it is neither too cold nor too hot.

解释：

"既……又……"表示同时具有两方面的性质或情况，连接两个动词、动词短语或者两个形容词、形容词短语。"既……又……"后面的一对词或短语的音节往往是相等的。

练习：

1. 用"既……又……"连接句子：
   (1) 文化中心　　　　　政治中心
   (2) 简单　　　　　　　清楚
   (3) 懂汉语　　　　　　懂英语
   (4) 有湖　　　　　　　有山
   (5) 科学工作者　　　　教育工作者

2. 用"既……又……"回答问题：

   例：A: 那里是不是只适合种棉花？
   　　B: 那里既适合种棉花，又适合种水稻。

   (1) A: 你们工厂是不是只生产电视机？
   　　B:
   (2) A: 从北京到上海是不是只能坐火车？
   　　B:
   (3) A: 你们去中国是不是只学习汉语？
   　　B:

四、不过　however; only; merely

1. 那里可参观的名胜古迹相当多，不过没有北京多。

   There are many scenic spots and historical sites worth going to there; however, not as many as in Beijing.

2. 他的中文讲得很好，不过，有时发音还不太正确。

   He speaks Chinese very well, however, sometimes his pronunciation is not perfect.

3. 你这次考得虽然不太好，不过比上次有些进步。

   You did not do very well this time in the examination; however, you have made progress.

4. A: 这个照像机五百元，您要买吗？

   This camera costs five hundred dollars. Do you want to buy it?

   B: 不买，我不过问问多少钱。

   No, I just wanted to ask about the price.

解释：

　　作为连词，"不过"表示转折，语气比"但是""可是"轻。作为副词，"不过"是"只是"的意思。

练习：

1．用"不过"回答问题：

例：A：那里夏天热不热？

B：那里夏天相当热，不过，没有北京热。

（1）那篇文章写得怎么样？

（2）你觉得这个电影有意思吗？

（3）那个地方气候怎么样？

（4）这个公园大不大？

（5）这篇文章是不是太难了？

（6）这座山高不高？

2．用"不过"改句子：

（1）我不会照像，只是照一张试试。

（2）周幽王叫人点烽火，只是为了让他的妻子笑一笑。

（3）隋朝修运河，当时只是隋炀帝为了坐船玩乐。

五、认识到……   to come to realize

例句：

1．我们跟他谈话以后，他已经认识到了自己的错误。

After we talked with him, he realized that he was wrong.

2．从过去的经验，我们认识到发展教育事业的重要。

From past experience, we have realized the importance of developing e-
ducation.

3．我们认识到只有发展生产，才能提高人民的生活水平。

We have realized that only by developing production can we raise the
people's living standard.

4．我们认识到，要学好英语，必须经常听、经常说。

We have realized that we must listen more and speak more if we want to
learn English well.

解释：

"认识到……"表示从经验、事实看出、懂得一个道理，总结出一个规
律性的东西。后面可以跟名词、动词短语或小句。

练习：

　　1. 用"认识到……"连接句子：

　　　　(1) 教育青年、热爱劳动

　　　　(2) 发展和各国人民的友好关系

　　　　(3) 接受别人的意见

　　　　(4) 大家的意见是对的

　　　　(5) 就会爆发农民起义

　　2. 用"认识到……"完成句子：

　　　　(1) 学习了两年汉语，我认识到＿＿＿＿＿＿＿＿＿＿＿＿＿。

　　　　(2) 吸取了过去的教训，他认识到＿＿＿＿＿＿＿＿＿。

　　　　(3) 研究了几年中国历史，我认识到＿＿＿＿＿＿＿＿。

　　　　(4) 这个青年在工厂工作了几年，他认识到＿＿＿＿＿＿＿。

六、要……必须……　　in order to... must...

例句：

　　1. 要了解世界大事，必须每天看报。

　　　　In order to know what is happening in the world, one must read newspapers every day.

　　2. 要有健康的身体，必须经常锻炼。

　　　　Only through regular physical exercise can one keep fit.

　　3. 要研究中国文学，必须懂一点中文。

　　　　If you want to do research on Chinese literature, you have to learn some Chinese.

解释：

　　"要……必须……"的主语是泛指的，所以省去。第一分句"要……"前也省去了表示条件和假设的连词"要是""如果"等。这种句子的格式是："要A（达到某一目的）必须B（这样做）"。

练习：

　　1. 用"要……必须……"改句子：

　　　　例：只有经常复习才能巩固学过的东西。

　　　　　　→要巩固学过的东西，必须经常复习。

　　　　(1) 只有自己去试试才能学会开机器。

(2) 只有了解人民的生活，才能写出人民喜欢的作品。

(3) 只有了解了唐朝的历史，才能更好地研究唐朝的诗歌。

(4) 只有团结起来，才有强大的力量。

(5) 只有学好中文，才能了解中国的文化。

2. 完成句子：

(1) 要发展农业生产，必须＿＿＿＿＿＿＿＿＿＿＿＿＿＿＿＿＿。

(2) 要让国家强大起来，必须＿＿＿＿＿＿＿＿＿＿＿＿＿＿＿。

(3) 要互相了解，必须＿＿＿＿＿＿＿＿＿＿＿＿＿＿＿＿＿。

(4) 汉武帝认识到要＿＿＿＿＿＿＿＿＿＿＿＿＿＿＿＿，必须打通去西域的路。

(5) 要让学生＿＿＿＿＿＿＿＿＿＿＿＿＿＿＿＿＿，必须举个例子来说明一下。

七、整＋〔量〕（〔名〕）　whole＋M（N）

例句：

1. 他整天坐在图书馆里看书。

He stays in the library reading all day long.

2. 他整年整月不在家，不是到上海去，就是到广州去。

He if frequently out of town, if he does not go to Shanghai then he goes to Guangzhou.

3. 为了早点把那篇文章翻译出来，昨天晚上他整夜没睡。

In order to finish translating that article earlier, he stayed up all night last night.

4. 他看小说看得真快，不到三个小时就把那一整本书看完了。

He reads so fast that he finished that novel in less than three hours.

5. 这篇文章他写了一整天。

He has spent the whole day writing this article.

解释：

"整"和表示时间的名词"年、月、天、夜"等结合，作状语，表示这一单位时间里，下面的动作或情况持续不断，往往带有一定的夸张的语气。"整"在"年、天、夜"自身兼有量词作用的名词前，前面可加数词，作动词的动量补语。如："用了两整天""谈了一整夜"。但"月"字不能这么用，只能说"整一个月""整两个月"。

和其他量词结合，"整"前也可以加数词，如"一整本书""一整套唱片""两整盒糖"。这时"（一）＋整＋［量］"作定语，修饰后面的名词，形容完整无缺。

练习：
    1．用"整天"或者"整年""整月""整夜"和下面的词语造句：
      （1）在外面跑   （4）吃喝玩乐
      （2）忙什么   （5）不休息
      （3）研究   （6）春秋战国时期、打仗
    2．用"一整天（年、夜）"回答：
      （1）你写这本小说用了多长时间？
      （2）你在车上坐了多久？
      （3）前十课你复习了多长时间？

八、不再……　no longer

例句：
    1．我上中学时很喜欢打球，上大学以后因为学习比较忙，就不再打球了。
    When I was a high school student, I liked playing ball games. But after I went to college, I no longer played for I was rather busy.
    2．黄河治理好了以后，不再发生水灾了。
    There was no longer flooding after the Yellow River was brought under control.
    3．汉武帝打败了匈奴，匈奴有很多年不再来侵扰。
    After the Huns were defeated by Emperor Wudi of the Han Dynasty, they did not attack for many years.
    4．做听写练习时，老师说："我只念三遍，念完三遍就不再念了。"
    In the dictation, the teacher said: "I am going to read only three times and I will not repeat anymore."

解释：
    "不再……"表示过去的动作或情况，以后不重复发生。"不再……"后面的动词可以指过去时间的事，如例 1、2、3。也可以指未来时间的事。如例 4。在口语里，句尾常加表示情况发生变化的语气助词

"了"。

练习：
用"不再……"回答问题：
例：A：你明天跟我们一起去颐和园吗？
　　B：我去过两次，不再去了。
1. A：你现在还常常唱歌吗？
　 B：
2. A：他现在还常写诗吗？
　 B：
3. A：他毕业以后自己有了工作，还靠他母亲生活吗？
　 B：
4. A：参加锻炼以后，他还常生病吗？
　 B：
5. A：春秋时期，很多诸侯国的势力强大起来，他们还听周朝的
　　 话吗？
　 B：

听力练习

（听录音，听力问题见本书附录）

回答问题

1. 请你简单地说一说为什么汉武帝能把匈奴打败？
2. 古代的西域说的是什么地方？为什么把汉朝通西域的路叫做"丝绸之路"？
3. 请你讲一讲王昭君的故事。
4. 为什么说《史记》既是伟大的历史著作，又是优秀的文学著作？
5. 请你简单地说一说三国时期中国的政治情况。
6. 隋朝为什么那么快就灭亡了？请你把情况说一说。

7. 为什么中国人也叫做"汉人"或者"唐人"？

8. 唐朝的时候，中国文化发展得特别快，这和唐太宗有什么关系？

9. 请你把唐朝衰落的原因讲一讲。

10. 请你介绍两位唐朝杰出的诗人。

翻译练习

（英译汉，答案见本书附录）

1. a powerful and prosperous period
2. powerful tribes
3. to send soldiers to fight
4. to defeat the invading enemies
5. to have contact for a long time
6. cannot get through on the phone
7. to have trade relations with all the countries in the world
8. to use silk to make clothes
9. not understanding that policy
10. to explain with an example
11. to hand down to present
12. the original situation
13. previously did not know
14. She married a worker.
15. to promote friendly relations
16. records on floods
17. famous historical figures
18. biography of a philosopher
19. the image of a peasant
20. vivid image
21. to vividly describe
22. a lively style with substantial content
23. an outstanding historical work
24. a figure during the last years of Eastern Han Dynasty

25. divided into three states
26. the transportation on the canal
27. brought disaster
28. the leader of the delegation
29. to attend as a representative of the whole school
30. a powerful and prosperous country
31. to realize the importance of stability and unity
32. the merits of this work
33. opposing opinions
34. gradually declined
35. escaped in a great hurry
36. China has sent many delegations abroad to visit.
37. Friendly nations help each other in developing economy.
38. The leaders of the factory realize the importance of uniting with the workers.
39. When writing the biography of a historical figure one must pay attention to the creation of a vivid image.
40. The appearance of this problem strongly proves the importance of learning from history.
41. That outstanding philosophical work is vividly written as well as easy to understand.
42. As early as the Han Dynasty there was a monk who took light of travelling great distance to go on a pilgrimage to India for Buddhist scriptures.
43. What is the relation between the development of agriculture and the prosperity of the economy?
44. Please give an example to explain the situation.
45. He is an outstanding student representative and has attended many different types of conferences.
46. Where is the longest canal in the world?
47. After the enemies were defeated, they no longer raided our country.
48. To establish a powerful and prosperous country one must develop industry, commerce, agriculture, transportation, etc.
49. The country can prosper only with the new economic policy.
50. Last year there was flooding in the North, but the agricultrual production was not affected.

第 6 课

话说宋元明清

话说宋元明清

老师：我们已经把宋元明三个朝代和清朝初期的历史讲完了。今天我提几个问题复习复习，请同学们踊跃回答。

第一个问题：宋朝是哪年建立的？国都在哪儿？

玛丽：宋朝是公元960年建立的，国都在开封。

琳达：公元1127年以后，国都在现在的杭州。

老师：那么，你能谈谈宋朝迁都的原因吗？

琳达：宋朝是中国历史上外患最多的一个汉族政权。当时中国东北、西北部几个少数民族常常来侵扰，对宋朝的威胁很大。宋朝政治腐败，打不过这些少数民族，只好年年给人家送银子、丝绸。不过，这不能解决根本问题。公元1127年，北方少数民族政权金朝还是占领了开封，北宋就灭亡了。皇帝的一个弟弟逃到江南，在杭州又建立了一个国都。历史上把后来的这个宋朝叫南宋。

老师：南宋的建立，对南方经济发展起了什么作用？

汤姆：南宋建立以后，南方的农业得到了发展，手工业也更发达了，中国的经济中心从北方移到了南方。江南本来就是鱼米之乡，这时候就更繁荣了。

老师：南宋初期有一个著名的抗金英雄，他叫什么名字？

汤姆：岳飞。岳飞曾经带兵收复北方大片土地，一直打到开封附近。可是就在这时候，南宋皇帝听了宰相秦桧的话，在一天里一连下了十二次命令，强迫岳飞退兵。岳飞回到杭州不久，就被秦桧害死了。

老师：宋朝以后是哪个朝代？

彼得：好像是唐朝吧。

约翰：不对，唐朝在宋朝前面，宋朝以后是元朝。十二世纪末，北方蒙古人的势力越来越大，蒙古人先灭了金，又灭了南宋，统一了中国，建立了元朝。

老师：为什么元朝只统治了九十七年？

琳达：元朝统治者按照民族把人民分成四个等级，很不得人心，所以元朝只统治了九十多年，就被朱元璋领导的农民起义推翻了。朱元璋建立的朝代叫明朝。

老师：明朝的时候，中国在世界上的地位和对外关系怎么样？

玛丽：明朝的时候，中国是世界上一个富强的国家，农业、手工业、商业都非常发达，大城市有三十多个。海上交通也比较方便，和许多国家都进行贸易。明朝皇帝曾经派郑和带着很大的船队到南洋去。郑和在不到三十年的时间里，先后航海七次，到过南洋、印度洋十多个国家和地区，最远到过非洲。

老师：明朝是怎么灭亡的？

彼得：明朝末年，政治非常腐败，土地高度集中。有的地区十分之九的农民失去了土地，人民生活十分痛苦。

琳达：就这样，政府还要他们交税。为了活下去，各地农民纷纷起义，得到老百姓的拥护，农民领袖李自成打到北京时，明朝皇帝在一棵树上吊死了。这样，明朝的统治就结束了。

老师：讲得很清楚。谁接着谈谈，清朝是怎么建立的？

汤姆：当时中国东北地区的一个少数民族满族镇压了这次农民起义，开始了对中国的统治。

老师：清朝初期有一个皇帝叫康熙，为什么说他是一个有作为的皇帝？

约翰：康熙采取了一些恢复和发展社会生产的办法，使国家富强起来，人民生活也安定了。另外，他还平定了边疆地区的多次叛乱，制止了沙俄对东北的侵略，为清朝二百六十多年的统治打下了很好的基础。

老师：对！下面，哪位同学说说，宋元明清这四个朝代在文学上有什么主要成就？

玛丽：词这种诗歌形式，在宋代发展到了很高的水平。元朝时，戏曲流行，出现了大批元曲作家。明清时期的小说成就很大，像《三国演义》、《水浒传》、《西游记》和《红楼梦》等，在文学史上都有重要地位。

老师：今天大家回答得都很好，就复习到这里吧。下课！

1. **初期** chūqī（名）

   early period, initial stage

2. **踊跃** yǒngyuè（形）

   eager, enthusiastic

3. **迁都** qiāndū（动宾）

   to move the capital to another place

4. **外患** wàihuàn（名）

   foreign aggression

5. **威胁** wēixié（动、名）

   to threaten; menace

   ○ 岳飞的军队对北方的金是一个很大的威胁。

   The troops led by Yue Fei posed a great threat to the Jin in the North.

   ○ 汉朝初年，匈奴的力量很大，威胁着汉朝的统治。

   In the early years of the Han Dynasty the Huns were very powerful and threatened the Han Dynasty.

6. **腐败** fǔbài（形）

   corrupt, decayed

7. **打不过** dǎbuguò（动补）

   incapable of defeating

   ○ 汉武帝的时候，汉朝很强盛，匈奴打不过汉朝。

   In the time of the Emperor Wudi of the Han Dynasty, Han Dynasty was so powerful and prosperous that the Huns were unable to defeat it.

   ○ 南宋皇帝怕打过不金，就命令岳飞退兵。

   The emperor of the Southern Song Dynasty, fearing that the Jin could not be defeated, ordered Yue Fei to retreat.

   ○ 蒙古人的势力很大，打得过金。

   The military forces of the Mongols were so strong that they could defeat the Jin.

8. **银子** yínzi（名）

   silver

9. **根本** gēnběn（形、副）

fundamental; thoroughly

○ 明朝灭亡的根本原因是政治腐败。

The fundamental reason for the fall of the Ming Dynasty was political corruption.

○ 我根本没去过中国，当然没参观过故宫了。

I've never been to China, so of course I've never visited the Palace Museum.

○ 我姐姐根本不懂英文，你怎么给她买了本英文小说？

Why did you get my sister an English novel, when (you know) she knows absolutely no English.

10. 占领 zhànlǐng （动）

  to occupy

11. 手工业 shǒugōngyè （名）

  handicraft industry

12. 移 yí （动）

  to remove, to shift

13. 本来 běnlái （副）

  originally

14. 著名 zhùmíng （形）

  well-known

15. 抗（金） kàng （Jīn） （动）

  to resist （the Jin）

16. 英雄 yīngxióng （名）

  hero

17. 曾经 céngjīng （副）

  once, before

18. 收复 shōufù （动）

  to recover, to recapture

19. 附近 fùjìn （名）

  nearby, vicinity

20. 宰相 zǎixiàng （名）

  prime minister （in feudal China）

21. 一连 yīlián （副）

  in a row, in succession

22. 下命令 xià mìnglìng （动宾）

112

to send down an order

23. 强迫 qiǎngpò（动）

to force

24. 退兵 tuìbīng（动）

to retreat; the withdrawal of a military force

25. 害死 hàisǐ（动补）

to murder

26. 末年 mònián（名）

last years of a dynasty or reign

27. 等级 děngjí（名）

class, rank

28. 不得人心 bùdérénxīn

not enjoy popular support; unpopular

○ 杨贵妃和她哥哥做了许多不得人心的事，所以士兵都恨他们。

Because Lady Yang and her elder brother had done many things that were unpopular, all the soldiers hated them.

○ 元朝统治者把人民分成四个等级，很不得人心。

The rulers of the Yuan Dynasty divided the people into four classes and therefore were very unpopular.

○ 康熙采取了一些很得人心的办法，生产恢复得很快。

Emperor Kangxi adopted a few policies which were supported by the people; therefore, production was quickly recovered.

29. 推翻 tuīfān（动）

to overthrow

30. 对外关系 duìwài guānxi

foreign relations

31. 富强 fùqiáng（形）

prosperous and strong

32. 贸易 màoyì（名）

trade

33. 船队 chuánduì（名）

fleet

34. 先后 xiānhòu（副）

early or late; priority; one after another

35. 航海 hánghǎi（动）

navigation

36. **高度** gāodù （副、名）

a high degree of；highly；altitude，height

37. **失去** shīqù （动）

to lose

38. **痛苦** tòngkǔ （形、名）

pain，suffering

○ 秦始皇修长城给人民带来了极大的痛苦。

Emperor Qin Shihuang's construction of the Great Wall brought great suffering to the people.

○ 明朝末年人民生活很痛苦。

Toward the end of the Ming Dynasty people were suffering.

39. **交税** jiāo shuì （动宾）

to pay tax

40. **老百姓** lǎobǎixìng （名）

commoner，ordinary people

41. **拥护** yōnghù （动）

to support，to endorse

42. **棵** kē （量）

（measure word for plant）

43. **接着** jiēzhe （动、副）

to follow，to carry on；then

44. **镇压** zhènyā （动）

to oppress

45. **有作为** yǒu zuòwéi

to have achievement

○ 很有作为

to have had great accomplishment

○ 没有作为

to have accomplished nothing

○ 没什么作为

to have done something not worthwhile of mentioning

46. **采取** cǎiqǔ （动）

to adopt

47. **恢复** huīfù （动）

to restore, to renew, to regain

48. **使** shǐ（动）

to cause, to enable

49. **平定** píngdìng（动）

to put down, to calm down

50. **叛乱** pànluàn（名）

rebellion

51. **制止** zhìzhǐ（动）

to curb, to stop

52. **侵略** qīnlüè（动、名）

to invade; invasion

53. **打下基础** dǎxià jīchǔ

to lay foundation

○ 汤姆学过四年中文，为研究中国诗歌打下了基础。

Tom had four years of Chinese which laid the foundation for him to
study Chinese poetry.

○ 明清时期，小说成就很大，给中国后来的小说打下了很好的基础。

During the Ming and Qing periods, the writing of novels had attained
great success, which laid a solid foundation for future novels.

54. **成就** chéngjiù（名）

accomplishment, success

55. **词** cí（名）

a form of poetry writing, fully developed in the Song Dynasty

56. **形式** xingshì（名）

form, shape

57. **戏曲** xìqǔ（名）

traditional opera

58. **流行** liúxíng（动）

prevalent, fashionable

59. **大批** dàpī（形）

large quantities of

60. **作家** zuòjiā（名）

writer

61. **小说** xiǎoshuō（名）

novel, fiction

专　名

1. 宋	Sòng	the Song Dynasty
2. 开封	Kāifēng	Kaifeng
3. 金	Jīn	the Jin Dynasty
4. 江南	Jiāngnán	south of the Yangtze River
5. 岳飞	Yuè Fēi	Yue Fei
6. 秦桧	Qín Huì	Qin Hui
7. 朱元璋	Zhū Yuánzhāng	Zhu Yuanzhang
8. 郑和	Zhèng Hé	Zheng He
9. 南洋	Nányáng	an old name of Southeast Asia
10. 印度洋	Yìndùyáng	the Indian Ocean
11. 非洲	Fēizhōu	Africa
12. 李自成	Lǐ Zìchéng	Li Zicheng
13. 康熙	Kāngxī	Emperor Kangxi
14. 沙俄	Shā'É	Tsarist Russia
15. 三国演义	Sānguóyǎnyì	*The Romance of the Three Kingdoms*
16. 水浒传	Shuǐhǔzhuàn	*The Outlaws of the Marsh*
17. 西游记	Xīyóujì	*Journey to the West*
18. 红楼梦	Hónglóumèng	*A Dream of Red Mansions*

语言点和练习

一、曾经　once; before

例句:

1. 我曾经在上海住过三年。

I once lived in Shanghai for three years.

2. 他曾经学过一年汉语，现在又学日语了。

He once learned Chinese for a year. Now he is taking Japanese.

3. 郑和曾经到过非洲。

Zheng He once went to Africa.

4. 蒙古人曾经统治了九十七年。

The Mongols once ruled for ninety-seven years.

解释：

"曾经"表示从前有过某种行为，经历或情况。"曾经"后面的动词往往带"过"，有时带"了"。"曾经＋动词"的否定式是："没（有）＋动词＋过"，例如，"我没有学过英文"。

练习：

1. 填空：

(1) 我爸爸曾经_____日本，但是我妈妈_____日本。

(2) 我的朋友琳达曾经_____杭州西湖，她很喜欢那个地方。

(3) 我姐姐_____演员，你记错了吧！

2. 改正下列病句：

(1) 他曾经学过中文，我没曾经学过。

(2) 李刚曾经看《今天我休息》那个电影。

(3) 马老师昨天曾经来一次，你没在宿舍。

3. 用"曾经"完成对话：

(1) A：你哥哥当过工人吧？

   B：_____。

(2) A：开封是不是宋朝的国都？

   B：_____。

(3) A：听说明朝的郑和到过非洲？

   B：_____。

二、一直　straight；always

例句：

1. 你一直走，别拐弯儿。

Go straight ahead. Don't turn.

2. 一直往西走，就能走到天安门。

Go all the way to the west; you will get to the Tian'anmen Square.

3. 上海的工商业一直非常发达。

The industry and commerce in Shanghai have always been very prosperous.

4. 王昭君在匈奴那里一直生活了几十年。

Wang Zhaojun lived among the Huns for decades.

5. 我等了他一上午，他一直没来。

I waited for him for a whole morning, but he never showed up.

解释：

"一直"有两个意思：a）表示顺着一个方向不变，如例句1、2。b）表示动作始终不间断，或情况始终不改变，如例句3、4。它的否定式是："一直不（没有）＋动词"，表示动作或情况始终没有发生，如例句5。

练习：

1. 请说出下列句子里"一直"的意思有什么不同：

(1) 一直往前走就是博物馆。

(2) 大雨一直下了三天。

(3) 他工作一直很努力。

2. 用"一直"改写句子：

(1) 往南走不拐弯儿有一个商店。

(2) 他中学的时候学习很好，大学的时候学习也很好。

(3) 这课练习真难，我从八点做到十二点才做完。

3. 用"一直"完成对话：

(1) A：中国的民族那么多，他们能团结吗？

B：_____。

(2) A：汤姆对中国文化有没有兴趣？

B：_____。

(3) A：昨天晚上，你等了他多长时间？

B：_____。

(4) A：听说你不喜欢吃鸡。

B：_____。

三、一连   continuously; in a row; in succession

例句：

1. 那个电影真好，我一连看了两次。

That movie is just wonderful. I went to see it twice in a row.

2. 一连下了三天雨，今天早上才晴了。

It has been raining continuously for three days, and it only cleared up this morning.

3. 他身体很好，能一连工作十几个小时。

He is in very good shape, so he can work continuously for more than ten hours.

解释：

"一连"表示同一动作接连发生，同一情况接连出现，动词后常跟表示次数或时间的数量词。

练习：

1. 用"一连"完成下列句子：

(1) 汤姆在一天中_____。

(2) 那个电影_____。

(3) 上课的时候，老师_____。

2. 用"一连"完成对话：

(1) A: 这本小说很有意思吧？

　　B: _____。

(2) A: 这几天真冷啊！

　　B: _____。

(3) A: 今天你学习了几个小时？

　　B: _____。

(4) A: 昨天你是不是来找过我？

　　B: _____。

四、先……又……　first... then...

例句：

1. 他先让客人坐下，又倒了一杯菜。

First he asked the guest to sit down; then he poured a cup of tea.

2. 琳达先游览了杭州西湖，又坐火车到了苏州。

Linda first visited the West Lake in Hangzhou; then she went to Suzhou by train.

3. 明天我想先参观天安门广场，再参观故宫。

I think tomorrow I will visit Tian'anmen Square first, and then the Palace Museum.

解释：

"先……又……"表示动作先后承接。这里所说的"动作"，可以是两个动作的相继发生，如例句1、2。"先……又……"和"先……再……"不同，"先……又……"用于已实现的动作，"先……再……"用于未实现的动作，如例句3。

练习：

1. 用"先……又……"完成对话：

(1) A：今天上午你去哪儿了？

    B：＿＿＿＿＿＿＿＿＿＿＿＿＿＿＿＿＿。

(2) A：上星期你去公园了还是看电影了？

    B：＿＿＿＿＿＿＿＿＿＿＿＿＿＿＿。

(3) A：金和南宋是同时被蒙古人灭掉的吗？

    B：＿＿＿＿＿＿＿＿＿＿＿＿＿＿＿。

2. 选择填空（"先……又……"或"先……再……"）

(1) 请你＿＿＿＿念一遍生词，＿＿＿＿念一遍课文。

(2) 我想＿＿＿＿到邮局寄封信，＿＿＿＿去商店买点儿糖。

(3) 昨天晚上我＿＿＿复习了半小时课文，＿＿＿做了一小时练习，十一点才睡觉。

(4) 我问他会不会讲汉语，他＿＿＿＿＿＿说不会，＿＿＿＿＿＿说会一点儿。

(5) 你应该＿＿＿＿念生词，＿＿＿＿念课文。

3. 改正下列病句：

(1) 昨天我先到书店买了一本书，再到电影院看了一个电影。

(2) 你要先复习课文，又做练习。

(3) 我想先去上海，又去杭州。

五、进行　to go on; to carry on; in progress

例句：

1. 大会正在进行。

The conference is in progress.

2. 同学们正在进行复习。

The students are reviewing their lessons.

3. 对这件事，我们还要进行研究。

We need to carry on further discussion of this matter.

解释：

"进行"这个词可以单独使用，如例句1，后面也可以带宾语。如果带宾语，这个宾语多是双音节动词。"进行"后面的动词不能重叠，也不能带其他成分，如例句2、3。另外，"进行"后面的宾语不能是动宾结构或动补结构的双音节动词，如不能说"进行吃饭""进行推翻"等。

练习：

1. 熟读以下短语：

进行贸易　　进行镇压　　进行侵略

进行研究　　进行教育　　进行统治

2. 选用练习1中短语完成下列句子：

(1) 沙俄曾经对中国东北_____。

(2) 孩子们做了错事，老师要对他们_____。

3. 模仿造句：

(1) 中国人民对黄河进行了长期治理。

(2) 金对北京进行过多次侵扰。

六、不到　less than；not yet

例句：

1. 在不到三年的时间里，他就学会了汉语。

He has learned to speak Chinese in less than three years.

2. 他今年还不到二十岁呢。

He is less than twenty years old.

3. 我八点钟上课，现在到八点了吗？

I have class at 8 o'clock. It is not yet 8 o'clock, is it?

解释：

"不到"中的"到"字，在这里的意思是"达到"。"不到"（或"没到")的肯定式是"到（了）"。"到（了）""不到""没到"的前面或后面常常有数量词。

练习：

1. 选择填空："到了""不到""没到"
   (1) 我爸爸还_____四十，可是头发已经白了。
   (2) 上课的时间_____，快走吧！
   (3) _____明朝后期，政治非常腐败。
   (4) 元朝_____一百年就灭亡了。

2. 用"到了"或"不到"改写句子：
   (1) 我五十五分钟就做完了练习。
   (2) 小明今年刚十三岁半，可是长得像大人一样高。
   (3) 快开演了，我们进去吧！

3. 用"不到"完成对话：
   (1) A：请问，现在几点了？
       B：_____
   (2) A：我们去上课吧！
       B：_____
   (3) A：你在公园玩了多长时间？
       B：_____

七、先后　early or late; priority; in succession

例句：

1. 琳达先后到过北京、西安等城市。
   Linda first went to Beijing and afterwards to Xi'an and other cities.

2. 北京先后做过元、明、清的国都。
   Beijing was successively the capital of the Yuan, Ming and Qing dynasties.

3. 汤姆先后三次参观故宫。
   Tom visited the Palace Museum three times.

4. 这本小说我先后看过两遍。
   I have read this novel twice.

122

解释:

"先后"在这里是副词,表示一段时间内事件发生的顺序,在句子中作状语。如果动词带数量词,语序有如下两种:

a)先后 + 数量词 + 动词。如例句3。

b)先后 + 动词 + 数量词。如例句4。

练习:

1.用"先后"改写句子:

(1)西安作过汉朝的国都,也作过唐朝的国都。

(2)蒙古人先灭了金,后来又灭了南宋。

(3)我星期一开了一次会,星期三开了一次会,星期五又开了一次会。

(4)唐代杰出的诗人很多,先出现了李白,又出现了杜甫。

2.用"先后 + 动词"或"先后 + 动词 + 数量词"(先后 + 数量词 + 动词)这样的格式填空:

(1)黄帝以后,_____尧、舜、禹三位著名领袖。

(2)战国时期,秦始皇_____国家,统一了中国。

(3)我的朋友_____我到他家吃饭,因为太忙,我只去过一次。

(4)郑和_____航海,到过许多国家和地区。

八、接着 to follow; to carry on; to continue

例句:

1.今天客人真多,一个接着一个。

Today we have had so many guests, one after another.

2.他念完以后,请你接着念。

Please continue to read when he finishes reading (his part).

3.他讲得很对,我想接着他的话再说几句。

What he has said is correct. I would just like to add a few words.

解释:

"接着"可以作谓语,表示两个事物的连接,如例句1。也可以作状语,表示后面和前面的动作在时间上连接得很紧,如例句2、3。

练习:

1.模仿造句:

（1）她下了课接着就回宿舍了。
（2）街上的汽车很多，一辆接着一辆。
（3）他念完请你接着念。
（4）宋朝灭亡以后，接着是元朝。

2．用"接着"和指定的词语完成对话：

（1）A：你这几天很忙吗？

B：_____。（一件）

（2）A：宋朝后面是哪个朝代？

B：_____。（元朝）

（3）A：唐朝的士兵杀死杨贵妃的哥哥以后，杨贵妃怎么样了？

B：_____。（上吊）

（4）A：老师，黄河流域讲完了吧？明天讲什么？

B：_____。（长江流域）

九、使　to cause; to enable

例句：

1．明朝后期土地高度集中，使大部分农民失去了土地。

In the later period of the Ming Dynasty, the land was highly central-ized, which caused most of the peasants to lose their land.

2．南宋的建立使南方的经济繁荣起来。

After the establishment of the Southern Song Dynasty, the economy in the South was booming.

3．这次旅行，使琳达进一步了解了中国。

Linda has a better understanding of China after this trip.

解释：

课文中的"使"，意思是"叫""让""致使"。在绝大多数情况下，带"使"的句型是："使＋谁（或什么）＋动词"。这里的"谁"或"什么"，一定是"使"的对象，同时又是后面动词的主体。

练习：

1．熟读下列短语：

使国家富强起来　　　　使政权巩固

使人民生活安定　　　　使农民失去土地

使经济繁荣　　　　　　　　使社会发生重大变化

2.选择练习 1 中的短语完成句子：

(1) 康熙采取了一些发展生产的办法，_____。

(2) 唐玄宗以后，经过八年战争，_____。

听力练习

（听录音，听力问题见本书附录）

回答问题

1. 宋朝为什么迁都？迁都以后对中国经济的发展有什么影响？
2. 请你讲一讲抗金英雄岳飞的故事。
3. 岳飞被害死了，这对宋朝以后的发展有什么影响？
4. 元朝在开始的时候力量很强，为什么只统治了九十多年就灭亡了？
5. 明朝的对外关系有什么可说的地方？
6. 明朝在中国的历史上有什么特点？
7. 明朝的统治是因为李自成打到北京结束的，可是，为什么建立新朝代的统治者不是李自成？
8. 清朝初年国家富强的原因是什么？
9. 请你介绍一下中国文学在宋朝以后的发展情况。
10. 谈谈宋、元、明、清四朝在经济方面的发展。

翻译练习

（英译汉，答案见本书附录）

1. to be very active during the early period
2. to participate eagerly
3. moved the capital twice

4. foreign invasion from the North
5. was threatened by the Huns
6. to solve the essential problem
7. the way to solve it
8. during the enemy occupation
9. to develop handicrafts
10. to move the industrial center to the West
11. heroic figures in history
12. to have happened before
13. to recover lost territory
14. hotels near the capital
15. a famous imperial prime minister
16. Three people died one after another.
17. to be forced to retreat
18. to force others to participate
19. to be divided into several classes
20. to promote foreigh relations
21. The program is on.
22. to carry out cultural exchange
23. to promote trade
24. to learn the techniques of navigation
25. industry is highly centralized
26. the pain of losing one's parents
27. the relationship between the government and the people
28. the policy that is supported by the people
29. to end the period of disunity
30. a capable leader
31. to adopt a new economic policy
32. to restore friendly relations
33. to stop the invasion of the enemies
34. to lay the foundation for future development
35. achievements in literature
36. to use the form of traditional opera
37. a large quantity of novels in translation
38. Traditional operas were very popular in the Yuan Dynasty.

39. Poetry has always been a well accepted literary form.

40. At present which folk song is the most pupular?

41. In recent years many outstanding young writers appeared in Taiwan.

42. Among all these questions, which is the most essential?

43. Which emperor of the Qing Dynasty first defeated the enemy and then put down the domestic rebellion?

44. The peasants lost their land and their life became harder and harder with each day.

45. New economic policy allowed commerce to develop to a high level.

46. I placed three calls, but not even a single one went through.

47. In less than a year after that area was occupied, the economy became damaged.

48. The basic problem cannot be solved if the original method is reintroduced.

49. That ruler first solved the problem of the high concentration of land, and then changed the old agricultural policies.

50. A stable and prosperous society enables the young people to have a chance to achieve success.

第 7 课

纪念碑前话百年

纪念碑前话百年

（一位导游和几位游客来到天安门广场人民英雄纪念碑前，导游向游客做介绍。）

各位朋友，这座高大的石碑叫人民英雄纪念碑。大家看，石碑的四周都是浮雕。这些浮雕记载了中国近代一百多年的历史。现在，我把这些浮雕给大家介绍一下。

第一幅是"虎门销烟"。十八世纪后期，为了掠夺中国财富，英国商人把大批鸦片卖到中国，给中国带来了灾难。清朝大臣林则徐主张禁止鸦片。他命令外国商人交出鸦片，然后把鸦片全部销毁了。大家看，这就是虎门销烟时的情况。

因为销烟的事，英国就在一八四〇年对中国发动了侵略战争。清朝在战争中失败了。一八四二年八月，英国强迫清政府签订了"南京条约"。后来，法国、美国、日本、俄国等也强迫中国签订了一些不平等条约。从这以后，中国慢慢变成了一个半殖民地半封建社会。

第二幅浮雕是"太平天国"。鸦片战争以后，人民生活更痛苦了。战后十年，全国爆发过一百多次农民起义，其中最大的是洪秀全领导的太平天国起义。他们的目的是推翻清朝统治，赶走外国侵略者。大家看，浮雕上那些手拿武器的农民，就是英勇的起义战士。他们曾经在南京建立政权，一直战斗了十四年。后来，在清政府和外国侵略者的联合镇压下失败了。

后面这幅是"武昌起义"。武昌起义发生在一九一一年十月十日，这一年是旧历辛亥年，所以这次革命就叫辛亥革命。辛亥革命的领导人是孙中山，革命纲领是三民主义。这次革命推翻了清朝，结束了中国两千多年的君主制，建立了中华民国。但是它并没有完成反帝反封建的历史任务，所以孙中山临终前说："革命尚未成功，同志仍须努力。"

接着的一幅是"五四运动"。辛亥革命爆发不久，北洋军阀夺取了政权。第一次世界大战结束，中国也是战胜国，德国在中国山东的特权本来是应该废除的，可是军阀政府在帝国主义者压力下却要把这特权交给日本。这样，五四运动就爆发了。一九一九年五月四日，北京的学生们到天安门广场集会。大家看，这位男学生正在讲演，这位女学生正在散发传单。全国人民都支持学生运动，结果，军阀政府就没敢在对德和约上签字。后来，五四运动向新文化运动的方向发展，它举起的"科学""民主"两面大旗，对中国社会产生了深远的影响。

西面这幅是"八一起义"。五四运动以后，马克思主义开始在中国传播，一九二一年七月一日中国共产党成立了。一九二四年，共产党和孙中山领导的国民党合作，一起北伐，打败了北洋军阀。不久孙中山去世了，国民党的主要领导人违背了孙中山"联俄、联共、扶助农工"的三大政策，排斥和打击中国共产党人。在这种情况下，共产党人就在一九二七年八月一日发动了南昌起义。起义后，他们在朱德领导下，上了江西井冈山。在那里，朱德和毛泽东一起建立了革命根据地和中国工农红军。

下一幅是"游击战争"。一九三一年九月十八日，日本对中国发动了侵略战争。他们先占领了中国东北，然后想再占领全中国。一九三四年十月到一九三五年十月，共产党领导工农红军经过两万五千里长征，从江西来到北方抗日前线。为了抗日，共产党和国民党第二次合作，并且建立了许多根据地，组织人民进行游击战争。大家看，浮雕上的男女农民拿着武器，正准备去和敌人战斗。一九四五年八月，中国人民终于把日本侵略者赶出了中国。

最后这幅最大的浮雕叫"胜利渡江"。抗日战争胜利后，中国又进行了三年内战。中国的解放战争是从一九四六年开始的。战争开始不到三年，解放军就解放了长江以北的大半个中国。一九四九年四月，解放军开始渡长江。大家看，这些战士已经上岸，正向南京冲去，后面的千万只战船在前进。二十一日南京解放，蒋介石和他的军队退到了台湾。十月一日，中华人民共和国就成立了。

生　　词

1. **导游** dǎoyóu（名）
   tour guide
2. **游客** yóukè（名）
   tourist
3. **石碑** shíbēi（名）
   stone tablet
4. **四周** sìzhōu（名）
   all around
5. **浮雕** fúdiāo（名）
   relief（sculpture）
6. **近代** jìndài（名）
   modern times
7. **幅** fú（量）
   （for paintings, etc.）piece
8. **销烟** xiāoyān（动宾）
   to destroy the opium
9. **掠夺** lüèduó（动）
   to plunder, to pillage
10. **财富** cáifù（名）
    wealth
11. **鸦片** yāpiàn（名）
    opium
12. **大臣** dàchén（名）
    minister（of a monarchy）
13. **主张** zhǔzhāng（动、名）
    to advocate, to stand for; view
    ○ 学生们主张废除德国在山东的特权。
    The students maintained that the privileges held by Germany in Shandong Province should be abolished.
    ○ 孙中山先生主张和共产党合作。
    Mr. Sun Zhongshan advocated to collaborate with the Communist Par-

132

ty.

○ 我支持他们的主张。

I support their proposition.

14. 禁止 jìnzhǐ（动）

to prohibit, to ban

15. 然后 ránhòu（副）

afterwards

○ 老张喝了一口茶，然后对我说："请你等一下儿。"

Lao Zhang drank some tea and then said to me, "Please wait for a moment."

○ 我们先复习第六课，然后再学第七课。

We will review lesson 6 first, afterwards, we will study lesson 7.

○ 应该先学生词，然后才能看懂课文。

One should learn the new words first and only then can one understand the text.

16. 发动 fādòng（动）

to launch, to mobilize

17. 战争 zhànzhēng（名）

war

18. 签订 qiāndìng（动）

to conclude and sign（a treaty, etc.）

19. 条约 tiáoyuē（名）

treaty

20. 平等 píngděng（形）

equal; equality

21. 目的 mùdì（名）

purpose, objective

22. 赶走 gǎnzǒu（动补）

to drive away

23. 武器 wǔqì（名）

weapon

24. 战士 zhànshì（名）

soldier, fighter

25. 战斗 zhàndòu（动、名）

to fight; battle

26. 旧历 jiùlì（名）
　　the lunar calendar

27. 辛亥年 xīnhàinián（名）
　　the year of Xinhai（specif. 1911）

28. 革命 gémìng（名）
　　revolution

29. 纲领 gānglǐng（名）
　　guiding principle

30. 君主制 jūnzhǔzhì（名）
　　monarchy

31. 反帝反封建 fǎndì fǎnfēngjiàn
　　anti-imperialism and anti-feudalism

32. 任务 rènwù（名）
　　mission, task

33. 临终 línzhōng
　　on one's deathbed, just before one dies

34. 尚未 shàngwèi（副）
　　not yet; remain to be

35. 仍（须）réng（xū）（副）
　　（must）still

36. 军阀 jūnfá（名）
　　warlord

37. 夺取 duóqǔ（动）
　　to seize

38. 战胜国 zhànshèngguó
　　victorious nation

39. 特权 tèquán（名）
　　privilege

40. 废除 fèichú（动）
　　to abolish

41. 集会 jíhuì（动）
　　to hold a mass rally

42. 讲演 jiǎngyǎn（动、名）
　　to lecture; speech

　　演讲 yǎnjiǎng（动、名）

to lecture; speech

○ 他的讲演虽然短，可是很有意思。

Although his speech was not long, it was very interesting.

○ 在联合国演讲的中国代表是谁？

Who was the Chinese delegate that gave the talk at the United Nations?

43. 散发 sànfā（动）

　　to distribute, to send forth

44. 传单 chuándān（名）

　　leaflet

45. 支持 zhīchí（动、名）

　　to support; support

46. 和约 héyuē（名）

　　peace treaty

47. 签字 qiānzì（动宾）

　　to sign, to affix one's signature

48. 深远 shēnyuǎn（形）

　　far-reaching

49. 传播 chuánbō（动）

　　to disseminate, to spread

50. 旗 qí（名）

　　flag, banner

51. 成立 chénglì（动）

　　to establish

52. 合作 hézuò（动、名）

　　to cooperate; collaboration

○ 在工作中，他俩一直合作得很好。

They have always worked very well together.

○ 他们的合作非常成功。

Their collaboration was very successful.

53. 去世 qùshì（动）

　　to pass away, to die

54. 违背 wéibèi（动）

　　to disobey

55. 排斥 páichì（动）

　　to repel, to exclude

56. 打击 dǎjī （动、名）

to strike; attack

○ 团结起来打击侵略者。

Unite and fight against the invaders.

○ 他受过一次很大的打击。

He has suffered a tremendous blow.

57. 根据地 gēnjùdì （名）

base area

58. 游击战争 yóujī zhànzhēng

guerrilla war

59. 前线 qiánxiàn （名）

frontline

60. 组织 zǔzhī （动、名）

to organize; organization

○ 明天学校要组织我们游览长城。

Tomorrow the school is going to organize a sightseeing trip to the Great Wall for us.

○ 一个日本的体育组织要来访问。

A Japanese sports organization is coming to visit.

61. 终于 zhōngyú （副）

at (long) last; finally

○ 冬天过去了，春天终于来了。

The winter is over and spring has finally arrived.

○ 老师讲了三遍，我终于明白了。

After the teacher explained it three times, I finally understood.

62. 内战 nèizhàn （名）

civil war

63. 渡江 dùjiāng （动）

to cross a river

64. 以（北） yǐ（běi）（介）

to the（north of）

65. 冲 chōng （动）

to charge, to rush

66. 千万（只） qiānwàn（zhī）（数）

innumerable（thousands and thousands）

专　名

1. 人民英雄
纪念碑　　　Rénmín Yīngxióng
Jìniànbēi　　　the Monument to the People's Heroes

2. 林则徐　　　Lín Zéxú　　　Lin Zexu

3. 虎门　　　Hǔmén　　　Humen

4. 半殖民地
半封建社会　bàn zhímíndì
bàn fēngjiàn shèhuì　semi-feudal, semi-colonial society

5. 太平天国　　Tàipíngtiānguó　　the Taiping Heavenly Kingdom

6. 洪秀全　　　Hóng Xiùquán　　Hong Xiuquan

7. 武昌　　　Wǔchāng　　Wuchang

8. 孙中山　　　Sūn Zhōngshān　　Sun Zhongshan（Sun Yat-sen）

9. 三民主义　　Sānmín Zhǔyì　　the Three People's Principles

10. 中华民国　　Zhōnghuá Mínguó　　the Republic of China

11. 五四运动　　Wǔ-sì Yùndòng　　the May Fourth Movement

12. 新文化运动　Xīn Wénhuà Yùndòng　　the New Culture Movement

13. 马克思主义　Mǎkèsī Zhǔyì　　Marxism

14. 中国共产党　Zhōngguó Gòngchǎndǎng　the Chinese Communist Party

15. 国民党　　　Guómíndǎng　　Kuomintang, the Nationalist Party

16. 北伐　　　Běifá　　the Northern Expedition

17. 北洋军阀　　Běiyáng Jūnfá　　the Northern Warlords

18. "联俄、联共、
扶助农工"
三大政策　"liánÉ, liánGòng, fúzhù
nónggōng"
sān dà zhèngcè　the Three Great Policies of alliance
with Russia, cooperation with the
Communist Party and assistance to the
peasants and workers

19. 南昌　　　Nánchāng　　Nanchang

20. 朱德　　　Zhū Dé　　Zhu De

21. 毛泽东　　　Máo Zédōng　　Mao Zedong（Mao Tsetung）

22. 江西　　　Jiāngxī　　Jiangxi（Province）

23. 井冈山　　　Jǐnggāngshān　　Jinggang Mountains

24. 中国工农红军　Zhōngguó
GōngNóng Hóngjūn　the Chinese Workers'and Peasants'
Red Army

25. 抗日（战争）	Kàng Rì (Zhànzhēng)	(the War of) Resistance Again-st Japan
26. 两万五千里长征	Liǎngwàn-wǔqiānlǐ Chángzhēng	the 25, 000-*li* Long March
27. 中华人民 共和国	Zhōnghuá Rénmín Gònghéguó	the People's Republic of China

语言点和练习

一、在……中　in; during

例句：

1. 李华在工作中非常努力。
   Li Hua is very diligent in his work.
2. 在旅行中，琳达学到了许多东西。
   Linda has learned a lot during that trip.
3. 在学习中，小王对我的帮助很大。
   Xiao Wang was very helpful to me in my study.

解释：

这课的"在……中"指的是，在某个动作进行的时候。这一格式一般出现在书面语中。

练习：

1. 说出下面四个句子里"在……中"的意思有什么不同：
   (1) 在鸦片战争中，清朝失败了。
   (2) 小孙在一个月中给妈妈写了四封信。
   (3) 在新文化运动中，马克思主义开始在中国传播。
   (4) 在这些老师中，陈老师最年轻。

2. 用"在……中"的格式完成句子：
   (1) _____困难很多。
   (2) _____有问题可以去问老师。
   (3) _____根据地的许多农民都参加了战斗。

138

二、［动］＋成　 to turn into；to succeed in doing（something）

例句：

1. 玛丽把"北京"（Běijīng）念成了"Běijīn"。

   Mary pronounced "Beijing" as "Beijin".

2. 这本书我上个月才写成。

   I did not finish writing this book until last month.

3. 因为没买到票，电影没看成。

   Since I could not get the ticket, I was unable to see the movie.

4. 昨天只到了两个人，会没开成。

   Yesterday only two people came, so there was no meeting.

解释：

动词"成"常作结果补语，主要表示两种意思：a）变为、成为。它后面必须带宾语，如例句 1。b）动作的完成、实现，如例句 2。它的否定式是"没……成"，如例句 3、4。

练习：

1. 熟读带"成"的短语：

   变成　 分成　 写成　 看成　 没参观成

   （会）没开成　 （课）没上成　 没来成

2. 选择练习 1 中的短语填空：

   (1) 一八四二年以后，中国慢慢＿＿＿＿＿＿＿＿＿了半殖民地半封
   　　建社会。

   (2) 老师病了，今天的汉语课＿＿＿＿＿＿＿＿＿。

   (3) 因为下雨，西湖＿＿＿＿＿＿＿＿＿。

   (4) 今天考试的时候，我把"广州"＿＿＿＿＿＿＿＿＿＿了"广
   　　川"。

3. 选择练习 1 中短语完成会话：

   (1) A：昨天开会你为什么没来?

   　　 B：＿＿＿＿＿＿＿＿＿＿＿＿＿＿。

   (2) A：星期六晚上我正准备去看电影，来了一位朋友。

   　　 B：＿＿＿＿＿＿＿＿＿＿＿＿＿＿。

   (3) A：老师，"杭州西湖"这四个字我写得对吗?

B: 不对，＿＿＿＿＿＿＿＿＿＿＿＿＿＿＿＿＿＿。

三、在……下　under; with

例句:

1. 在刘明帮助下，小华的练习很快就做完了。

   With Liu Ming's help, Xiao Hua quickly finished doing his exercises.

2. 在清朝的镇压下，太平天国革命失败了。

   Under the suppression of the Qing Dynasty, the Taiping Revolution failed.

3. 在困难情况下，他还是完成了任务。

   Although he did it under difficult circumstances, he was able to complete the task.

解释:

"在……下"表示条件。能嵌入这一格式的大多是名词短语或带有定语的双音节动词。

练习:

1. 用"在……下"和下面的词语组成句子:

   (1) 老师的教育　　　　小华认识到自己错了

   (2) 秦朝统治　　　　　人民生活很痛苦

2. 判别下列句子正误，再把错误的句子改正过来:

   (1) 张明在学习下非常努力。

   (2) 王老师在教学上很认真。

   (3) 在鸦片战争后的十年上，爆发过一百多次农民起义。

   (4) 在中国共产党领导下，中国人民赶走了外国侵略者。

   (5) 在全国人民支持中，五四运动胜利了。

3. 用"在工作上""在老师帮助下""在学习中"各造一个句子。

四、并没（有）　not at all

例句:

1. 宋朝虽然年年给金送银子，但并没有解决根本问题，后来金还是把北宋灭了。

Although the Song Dynasty gave silver to the Jin Dynasty every year, it did not at all solve the basic problem; in the end the Jin Dynasty still defeated the Northern Song Dynasty.

2. 有人说老孙去过法国，老孙说他并没有去过。

Someone said that Lao Sun had been to France, but Lao Sun said he had never been to France at all.

3. 他虽然是中国人，但由于从小生活在国外，并不会说中国话。

Although he is a Chinese, he cannot speak Chinese because he grew up abroad.

4. 这个句子虽然长，但是并不难。

Although this sentence is long, it is not difficult at all.

解释:

"并"用在否定词"没有"或"不"前，加强否定语气，说明事实跟某种看法或一般看法不一样。

练习:

1. 用"并不"或"并没有"改写句子:

(1) 有人说这本小说很生动，我觉得不像他们说的那样好。

(2) 我以为约翰来过中国，可是他说他没来过。

(3) 他在美国住过四年，可是英语说得不是太好。

(4) 王昭君原来是一个宫女，不是公主。

2. 用"并不"或"并没有"完成下列对话:

(1) A: 你妈妈是法国人，你会讲法语吧?

    B: _____。

(2) A: 《水浒传》写的是宋朝的事，作者是宋朝人吗?

    B: _____。

(3) A: 这件事他是怎么知道的，你告诉过他吧?

    B: _____。

五、临   just before (something happens)

例句:

1. 你临睡前，要把窗户关好。

Close the windows before you go to bed.

2. 临下课以前，老师说下星期考试。

Just before the class was over, the teacher said that there would be an examination next week.

3. 我的朋友临走的时候，送了我一张照片。

My friend gave me a picture just before he left.

解释：

"临"常和其他动词或动词性结构组成短语，表明动作即将发生前的一段时间。如"临走""临睡""临来""临上火车"等。这种短语，后面常带"前""以前""的时候"等。

练习：

1. 用"临"和横线中指定的词语完成句子：

(1) 医生对我说："＿＿＿＿＿＿＿＿＿＿睡＿＿＿＿＿＿＿＿＿＿再吃一次药。"

(2) ＿＿＿＿＿＿＿吃午饭＿＿＿＿＿＿＿，老刘来了。

(3) ＿＿＿＿＿＿＿＿＿＿离开＿＿＿＿＿＿＿＿＿＿＿＿我买了两盒中国茶。

2. 用"临……"改写下列句子：

(1) 明朝皇帝是在李自成快进北京的时候吊死的。

(2) 我要走了，他交给我一封信。

(3) 琳达到中国来的前一天，买了一本中国地图。

六、以（北）   to the（north）of; used to show the boundary of（direction, time or quantity）

例句：

1. 长江以南雨水比较多。（方位界限）

The rainfall in the south of the Yangtze River is relatively heavy.

2. 长城以外的地方我都没去过。（方位界限）

I have not been anywhere north of the Great Wall.

3. 三点钟以前我来找你。（时间界限）

I will come to see you before three o'clock.

4. 这班学生都在二十岁以下。（数量界限）

All the students in this class are under twenty.

解释：

由"以"和"东、西、南、北、上、下、前、后、内、外"等组成的方位词，所表示的意思如下表：

	方位界限	时间界限	数量界限
以东	马路以东		
以西	马路以西		
以南	长江以南		
以北	长江以北		
以上	三层楼以上	五年以上	三十岁以上
以下	三层楼以下		三十岁以下
以前		2002 年以前	第十课以前
以后		2002 年以后	第十课以后
以内	长城以内	三天以内	一百以内（的数）
以外	长城以外		

练习：

1．请说说下列四组词的意思：

(1) 长江以南、长江以北

(2) 一个月以内、一个月以上

(3) 三十岁以上、三十岁以下

(4) 学校以内、学校以外

2．选择填空：

（"以上""以内""以东""以北""以外""以后"）

(1) 我们学校在体育馆_____。

(2) 马路_____都是北京大学的房子。

143

（3）我的练习一个小时_____可以作好。

（4）我们班百分之四十_____是女同学。

（5）玛丽说，她午饭_____回来。

听力练习

（听录音，听力问题见本书附录）

回答问题

1. 请你讲一讲鸦片战争的经过和结果。
2. 中国第一个不平等条约是什么条约？它有什么影响？
3. 太平天国革命产生的原因是什么？
4. 请你简单地讲一讲太平天国为什么失败了？
5. 为什么孙中山先生说，"革命尚未成功，同志仍需努力"？
6. 请你介绍一下五四运动的背景。
7. 请你说一说五四运动对中国社会的影响。
8. 请你讲一讲"八一起义"的意义。
9. 请你介绍一下抗日战争的经过。
10. 请你说一说近代中国历史上发生过的几件重大事情。

翻译练习

（英译汉，答案见本书附录）

1. the guide of the tour group
2. the tourists around the memorial
3. the study in modern world history
4. to plunder the wealth of other countries
5. the minister who banned the trading of opium

6. to advocate trading with all countries
7. and then send the soldiers
8. to start a war
9. to sign a Sino-Japanese treaty of friendship
10. to reach the goal of equality
11. to drive away the invading enemy
12. the weapons that are banned
13. the soldier that participated in the Liberation War
14. the industrial revolution of the 18th century
15. the guiding principles in the development of socialism
16. to overthrow the monarchy
17. to complete the democratic revolution
18. to support the proposition of anti-imperialism and anti-feudalism
19. The revolutionary task has not been completed.
20. said before leaving
21. the warlords that started the war
22. to abolish unequal treaties
23. to make a speech at the assembly
24. to distribute leaflets in the streets
25. the victorious nations that signed the peace treaty
26. to support the anti-war views
27. Those who oppose please raise your hand.
28. to generate a far-reaching influence
29. to spread revolutionary ideas
30. to disobey one's parents' wishes
31. to exclude those who opposed him
32. went to the frontline to fight
33. finally established a new regime
34. to charge the enemy
35. the wheat-producing areas north of the Yangtze River
36. The guide of the tour group explained the content of the relief to the tourists.
37. To burn the opium was not the fundamental way to abolish it.
38. In the 19th century British merchants sold opium to China to plunder China's wealth.

39. The warlords in the North instigated a war under the support of the old powers.
40. The work to repair the ancient buildings is being carried out.
41. Signing the peace treaty did not prevent that country from starting a war.
42. He has become a writer from an illiterate.
43. Although we have gained some achievements, we must still work conscientiously.
44. Places called "lands of fish and rice" are mostly located south of the Yangtze River as the weather there is warm and the rain is plentiful.
45. When Mr. Sun Zhongshan died the democratic revolution had not yet been completed.
46. The Chinese Communist Party organized the people and carried out guerrilla warfare.
47. The students attending the rally were opposed to the government's signing of the treaty.
48. The New Culture Movement had a great effect on the development of Chinese literature.
49. The aim of establishing this organization is to promote the international agricultural cooperation.
50. We support this proposition; however, we do not exclude other views.

第 8 课

你了解中国的政治制度吗?

你了解中国的政治制度吗？

（星期三，学校有个讨论会，内容是中国当代政治和政府组织。汤姆和约翰是东亚系四年级的学生，他们两个都要参加讨论会。星期二晚上，汤姆正在屋子里看书，约翰走了进来。）

约翰： 汤姆，你看什么书呢？

汤姆： 《中国概况》。

约翰： 明天的发言准备好了吗？

汤姆： 差不多了，你呢？

约翰： 早准备好了，明天我争取第一个发言！

汤姆： 那我先提两个问题考考你怎么样？

约翰： 你随便问好啦！

汤姆： 你说中国是一个什么样的国家？

约翰： 这还不好回答？社会主义国家嘛！

汤姆： 中国的社会主义有什么特点，你讲详细点好吗？

约翰： 好吧。一九二一年，中国成立了共产党。中国共产党信仰马克思主义，要在中国建立社会主义制度。他们领导中国人民进行了长期的革命斗争，终于在一九四九年，建立了中华人民共和国……

汤姆： 对不起，等一下！

约翰： 怎么啦？

汤姆： 依我看，历史背景就不用讲了。

约翰： 好，不讲就不讲。一九四九年十月一日，中华人民共和国成立了。中国是共产党领导的社会主义国家，实行人民代表大会制度，全国人民代表大会既是最高立法机关，又是最高权力机关。一九五四年，中国召开了

148

第一届全国人民代表大会，制定了中华人民共和国宪法。工人、农民和知识分子都是国家的主人，人和人的关系是平等的，国家、集体和个人的利益是一致的。人民的民主权利得到国家法律的保护。

汤姆：依我看，中国的民主和法制都还不够健全。

约翰：不过，你也要看到发展和变化。近年来，中国领导人特别重视民主和法制问题。我相信中国能成为高度文明、高度民主的国家。

汤姆：可是，中国是由一个党领导的国家，怎么能实现你说的高度民主呢？

约翰：不错，中国是一个党领导的国家，难道一个党领导的国家就不能实现高度民主吗？中国共产党代表了全中国各族人民的利益，中国人民享有广泛的民主权利。再说呀，中国还有很多民主党派。这些民主党派都拥护共产党的领导，在社会主义建设中做出了很大贡献。中国共产党对他们非常信任，和他们一起讨论国家大事。他们当中有些人还担任了国家领导职务，比如孙中山先生的夫人宋庆龄女士就当过全国人民代表大会常务委员会副委员长和国家副主席。

汤姆：这也是中国的一个特点吧。你再说说中国的根本任务是什么？

约翰：这要看什么时候了。建国初期，国家的根本任务是巩固政权，恢复经济，建立社会主义制度。经过几十年的努力，取得了不少经验，也有过不少教训。

汤姆：现在呢？

约翰：现在总结了过去的经验教训，国家决定把工作重点放在经济建设方面。中国的面貌现在已经发生了根本的变化，再过几十年，中国一定可以成为既有现代工业、现代农业，又有现代国防和现代科学技术的社会主义强国。

汤姆：实现和平统一，是中国当前政治生活中的一件大事。你对中国统一问题有什么看法？

约翰：这个问题中国领导人讲得很清楚。台湾自古以来就是中国领土的一部分，海峡两岸的中国人都是炎黄子孙。过去，由于人为的原因，台湾和祖国分离了。现在实现和平统一，是中国人民的共同愿望。我认识不少华侨，他们也都盼着自己的祖国早日统一。香港和澳门已经先后在 1997 年和 1999 年回归祖国，相信台湾问题不久也会解决的。

汤姆：（倒了两杯酒）我们两个都是中国人民的朋友，来，为他们的愿望早日实现，干杯！

约翰：好，干杯！

生　词

1. 当代 dāngdài（名）
   contemporary

2. 发言 fāyán（名、动）
   speech；to speak，to make a statement
   ○ 你的发言真精彩！
   Your speech is really marvellous.
   ○ 他正在讨论会上发言呢。
   He is taking the floor in the discussion.

3. 差不多 chàbuduō（形、副）
   similar；almost
   ○ 约翰的发言准备得差不多了。
   John is about to finish preparing his speech.
   ○ 这两幅画儿差不多。
   These two paintings are similar.
   ○ 参加讨论会的人差不多都来了。
   Almost all the participants of the discussion are here.

4. 争取 zhēngqǔ（动）
   to strive for
   ○ 我们要争取世界和平。
   We must strive for world peace.
   ○ 中国人民争取早日实现祖国的和平统一。
   The Chinese people are striving for an early realization of the peaceful unification of their country.
   ○ 这本小说我争取三天看完。
   I'll try to finish reading this novel in three days.

5. 考 kǎo（动）
   to examine，to give a test

6. 随便 suíbiàn（形、副）
   casual，informal；randomly
   ○ 你随便说吧！
   Just say anything you want!

○ 这个人说话太随便。

He makes remarks too casually.

7. 好（［＋动]) hǎo （＋V）（副）

　　　　　　easy（to do）

○ 这个问题好回答。

This question is easy to answer.

○ 那本书不好买。

That book is not easy to buy.

8. 社会主义 shèhuìzhǔyì（名）

　　　socialism

9. 信仰 xìnyǎng（动、名）

　　　to have faith in, to believe; faith, belief

10. 制度 zhìdù（名）

　　　system

11. 长期 chángqī（名）

　　　long term; over a long period

12. 斗争 dòuzhēng（名、动）

　　　struggle; to struggle against

13. 依我看 yī wǒ kàn

　　　as I see it

14. 背景 bèijǐng（名）

　　　background

15. 实行 shíxíng（动）

　　　to implement, to carry out

16. 立法 lìfǎ

　　　legislation

17. 机关 jīguān（名）

　　　organization, office

○ 立法机关　legislature

18. 权力 quánlì（名）

　　　power, authority

19. 召开 zhàokāi（动）

　　　to convene

20. 届 jiè（量）

　　　session

21. 制定 zhìdìng（动）

to draw up（a constitution）, to work out（a plan）, to make（laws）, to formulate（methods）

22. 宪法 xiànfǎ（名）

constitution

23. 知识分子 zhīshifènzǐ（名）

intellectual, the intelligentsia

24. 主人 zhǔrén（名）

master

25. 集体 jítǐ（名）

collective

26. 个人 gèrén（名）

individual（person）

27. 利益 lìyì（名）

benefit, interest

28. 一致 yīzhì（形）

identical, unanimous

○ 我和你的意见是一致的。

My opinion is the same as yours.

○ 他们俩的看法不一致。

Their views are different.

○ 大家一致选他当班长。

He was unanimously elected class monitor.

29. 权利 quánlì（名）

right

30. 法律 fǎlǜ（名）

law

31. 保护 bǎohù（动）

to protect

32. 法制 fǎzhì（名）

legal system

33. 够 gòu（副、形）

enough; adequate

34. 健全 jiànquán（形、动）

perfect; to perfect, to strengthen

35. 近（几年）来 jìn（jǐnián）lái（副）

   (in) recent (years); recently

36. 重视 zhòngshì（动）

   to attach importance to, to value

37. 成为 chéngwéi（动）

   to become

   ○ 中国一定能成为发达的国家。

   China will certainly become a well-developed country.

   ○ 他已经成为著名的作家了。

   He has already become a famous writer.

38. 文明 wénmíng（形）

   civilized; civilization

39. 由 yóu（介）

   by, of, from

40. 享有 xiǎngyǒu（动）

   to enjoy (rights, prestige, etc.)

   ○ 人民都享有管理国家大事的权利。

   All the people enjoy the right to supervise their government.

41. 广泛 guǎngfàn（形）

   extensive, widespread

   ○ 中国文化在亚洲有着广泛深远的影响。

   The influence of Chinese culture in Asia has been far-reaching.

42. 党派 dǎngpài（名）

   (political) party

43. 信任 xìnrèn（动、名）

   to trust; confidence

   ○ 领导只有得到人民的信任，才能有作为。

   A leader can be successful only when he is trusted by his people.

44. 当中 dāngzhōng（名）

   in the middle of, among

   ○ 他们当中有三个是华侨。

   There are three overseas Chinese among them.

   ○ 十个苹果当中有两个是坏的。

   Of the ten apples there are two bad ones.

   ○ 一年当中他到中国去了三次。

He went to China three times in one year.

45. **担任** dānrèn（动）

to assume the office of, to hold the post of

○ 明年谁担任学生会主席？

Next year who will be the chairman of the student union?

46. **职务** zhíwù（名）

post

○ 他在政府里担任重要的职务。

He holds an important post in the government.

47. **比如** bǐrú（连）

for example

48. **女士** nǚshì（名）

lady, madam; Ms.（a polite form for a woman married or unmarried）

49. **常务委员会** chángwù wěiyuán huì（名）

a standing committee

50. **副** fù（形）

deputy, vice-

○ 副校长

vice-president（of a college）

○ 副总理

vice-premier

○ 副经理

assistant manager

○ 副总统

vice-president

51. **委员长** wěiyuánzhǎng（名）

chairman of a committee

52. **主席** zhǔxí（名）

chairman

53. **重点** zhòngdiǎn（名）

key point

54. **总结** zǒngjié（名、动）

summary

○ 做总结

make a summary

○ 总结报告

summary report

55. **国防** guófáng （名）

national defense

56. **领土** lǐngtǔ （名）

territory

57. **海峡** hǎixiá （名）

strait

58. **过去** guòqù （名）

（in）the past

○ 我们不能忘记过去。

We must not forget the past.

○ 老李过去不在这儿住。

Lao Li did not live here before.

59. **人为的** rénwéide

man-made

60. **分离** fēnlí （动）

to separate

61. **共同** gòngtóng （形）

common

62. **愿望** yuànwàng （名）

hope, wish

63. **华侨** huáqiáo （名）

overseas Chinese

64. **盼（着）** pàn（zhe）（动）

to look forward to

65. **早日** zǎorì （副）

at an early date; sooner

○ 早日建成

to complete at an early date

○ 早日统一

to be united soon

○ 早日解决

to be solved quickly

66. 倒（酒） dào（jiǔ）（动）
    to pour（wine）
67. 干杯 gānbēi（动宾）
    to drink a toast

专　名

1. 东亚	Dōng Yà	East Asia
2. 中国概况	Zhōngguó Gàikuàng	*A Survey of China*
3. 全国人民代表大会	Quánguó Rénmín Dàibiǎo Dàhuì	the National People's Congress
4. 宋庆龄	Sòng Qìnglíng	Song Qingling
5. 香港	Xiānggǎng	Hong Kong
6. 澳门	Àomén	Macao

语言点和练习

一、随便（+［动］）好啦　to（do）whatever（you）want to（do）

例句：

1. 你随便问好啦。
   You can ask whatever you want to.
2. 您随便拿好啦。
   Take whatever you like.
3. 让他随便说好啦。
   He can speak informally.
4. 你就随便画一幅好啦。
   It doesn't matter, just draw any old picture.

解释：
"随便＋动词＋好啦"表示行为动作不受限制，怎么方便就怎么做，有
"没关系""无所谓"的意思。其中的动词多是单音节及物动词，动词
后边一般只带数量宾语（如例句4），而很少带其他成分。

练习：

1. 用"随便＋动词＋好啦"回答下列问题：
   (1) A：这些书我可以看吗？
       B：
   (2) A：我的行李放在哪儿？
       B：
   (3) A：这里的书我可以借吗？
       B：

2. 用"随便＋动词＋好啦"完成句子：
   (1) 桌子上有很多菜，_____。
   (2) 这辆自行车是我的，_____。
   (3) 什么歌儿都可以，_____。
   (4) 什么样子的衣服都行，_____。
   (5) 多少钱都可以，_____。

二、（这）还不……（吗）?　　**how could this（be）**

例句：

1. 这个问题那么容易，还不好回答？
   How could this simple question be difficult to answer?

2. 山那么陡，他又不小心，这还不摔下来？
   The mountain was so steep and he was so careless, how could he not fall?

3. 这个练习老师讲过了，还不会做？
   How could you not know how to do this exercise when the teacher has already explained it to us?

解释：

"（这）还不……（吗)?"是用反问的形式表示肯定的意思。往往表示"容易做到"或"肯定发生"。这种句子句尾语气词"吗"常常省略。

练习：

1. 用"（这）还不……（吗)?"改写下列句子：
   (1) 这个句子好做。

158

(2) 那本小说好借。

(3) 这个任务好完成。

(4) 这件事情很简单。

2. 用 "（这）还不……（吗）?" 回答问题：

(1) A: 这个字你会念吗？

   B:

(2) A: 这首歌儿你会唱吗？

   B:

(3) A: 这个句子好翻译吗？

   B:

(4) A: 我的汽车坏了，你能修好吗？

   B: (用 "容易")

(5) A: 请你给我画一幅画儿好吗？

   B: (用 "好办")

三、依（我）看 according to..., it seems to (me)

例句：

1. 依我看，这个问题好解决。

   It seems to me that this question is easy to solve.

2. 依老师看，这些都不是重点词。

   According to the teacher, none of these words is important.

3. 依我看，小李有小李的优点，小刘有小刘的优点。

   As I see it, Xiao Li and Xiao Liu each has his own merits.

4. 依你说，他们俩谁的看法对呢？

   Between the two of them, whose opinion do you think is the correct one?

解释：

"依 + [代]（[名]) + 看 (说)" 用在主语前，有停顿，表示按照某人的看法。

练习：

用 "依……看 (说)" 回答下列问题：

1. A: 依你看，谁去合适？

B：

2．A：依你看，谁的办法好？

B：

3．A：依你说，他们俩谁的汉语水平高？

B：

4．A：依你说，他们学习汉语的目的是什么？

B：

四、不 A 就不 A　　If not..., that is all right.

例句：

1．A：依我的，明天你就不要去了。

I think you should not go tomorrow.

B：不去就不去。

That is all right with me.

2．A：李华说，他以后不再来了。

Li Hua said he would not come again.

B：不来就不来吧，人家不愿意来，那有什么办法呢？

That is all right. Since he does not want to come, what can we do?

3．A：今天的比赛他不参加了。

He will not participate in today's competition.

B：不参加就不参加，这有什么了不起的。

That is all right. It is not important.

4．A：她长得不怎么好看。

She is not very pretty.

B：不好看就不好看，不好看我也喜欢她。

It does not matter, I like her anyway.

解释：

"不 A 就不 A"在对话中表示勉强同意对方的意见，或者表示一种无所谓的态度。A 是动词、动词短语或形容词。这一句型，句尾有时可带语气助词"吧"。

练习：

用"不 A 就不 A"完成下列对话：

160

1．A：那件事你就别说了。

    B：

2．A：怎么办呢？大家的意见不一致。

    B：

3．A：你不让他去，他有点儿不高兴。

    B：

4．A：我不相信你的话。

    B：

5．A：依我说，这件衣服你穿有点儿不合适。

    B：

五、没有 A 就没有 B　without A there will not be B

例句：

1．没有溪流就没有江河。

Rivers come from streams and brooks.

2．没有小麦就没有面包。

Without wheat there can not be bread.

3．没有大家的共同努力，就没有这么大的成就。

If we had not all worked so hard, we would not have had such a great success.

4．没有高山就没有平原。

Without mountain there would not be plain.

解释：

"没有 A 就没有 B"表示两种意思：a）A 是 B 的前提和条件，如例句 1、2、3。b）A 和 B 互为条件，如例句 4。

练习：

1．用"没有 A 就没有 B"改写下列句子：

  （1）有了牛，才有牛奶。

  （2）有了科学技术的现代化，才有工业和农业的现代化。

  （3）由于大家的关心，我才有幸福的生活。

  （4）有东才有西，有南才有北。

2．用"没有 A 就没有 B"完成下列句子：

(1) ＿＿＿＿＿＿＿＿＿，就没有森林（forest）。

(2) ＿＿＿＿＿＿＿＿＿，就没有鱼。

(3) 没有鸡蛋，＿＿＿＿＿＿；没有鸡，＿＿＿＿＿＿。

六、够　enough

例句：

1. 做这件事有三个人就够了。

   It takes only three people to do this work.

2. 每月五百块钱够（他）花了。

   Five hundred dollars a month is enough (for him).

3. 这幅画儿画得够好（的）了。

   The drawing of this painting is good enough.

4. 这个办法不够科学。

   This method is not scientific enough.

解释：

"够"表示达到某种数量或程度。肯定句常常带语气助词"了"。

练习：

1. 完成下列对话：

   (1) A：学完这本书，半年时间够吗？

   　　B：

   (2) A：一瓶酒够喝吗？

   　　B：

   (3) A：买汽车的钱你借够了吗？

   　　B：

   (4) A：他说得清楚不清楚？

   　　B：

2. 把肯定句改成否定句，把否定句改成肯定句：

   (1) 写一篇文章有两天时间够了。

   (2) 我们七个人，三间房子不够住。

   (3) 两瓶酒够他喝了。

   (4) 这件衣服洗得不够干净。

   (5) 这首诗写得够生动了。

162

七、近（几年）来　for the past（time duration）...

例句：

1. 近几天来，差不多天天下雨。

   It has been raining for several days.

2. 近几个月来，他的身体一直不太好。

   He has not been well for the past few months.

3. 近几年来，中国的经济发展比较快。

   For the past few years, the economy in China has developed rather rapidly.

4. 近百年来，中国历史发生了很大变化。

   China has gone through great changes in the last century.

解释：

"近……来"表示从过去到现在一段较短时间，一般在主语前边。

练习：

1. 用"近……来"和所给的词造句：

   (1) 天　　一天到晚　　忙

   (2) 月　　生活　　一直　　安定

   (3) 年　　出现　　大批　　优秀　　作家

   (4) 百年　　世界　　发生　　变化

2. 完成下列句子：

   (1) 近几天来，＿＿＿＿＿＿＿＿＿＿＿＿＿＿＿＿。

   (2) 近几个月来，＿＿＿＿＿＿＿＿＿＿＿＿＿＿。

   (3) 近几年来，＿＿＿＿＿＿＿＿＿＿＿＿＿＿＿。

听力练习

（听录音，听力问题见本书附录）

回答问题

1. 请你谈谈中国的社会主义有什么特点。
2. 中国共产党成立的原因是什么？
3. 请你说一说中国当代的政治制度和组织。
4. 请你谈一谈你对中国的民主和法制的看法。
5. 请你介绍一下中国共产党和其他民主党派的关系。
6. 中国共产党建国初期的根本任务是什么？
7. 再过几十年的努力，中国要成为一个什么样的国家？
8. 请你说一点儿你知道的关于台湾的情况。
9. 是什么人为的原因使台湾和中国大陆长期分离呢？这个问题怎么解决？
10. 香港和澳门是什么时候回归祖国的？

翻译练习

（英译汉，答案见本书附录）

1. to discuss current politics
2. to give one's opinion eagerly
3. Nearly all spoke.
4. to try to attend
5. not easy to prepare for
6. different social systems
7. a long-term task
8. ideological struggle
9. I don't think it will be a problem.
10. historical background
11. to carry out socialism
12. the jurisdiction of the legislature
13. to convene the first session of the People's Congress

14. to implement the constitution
15. the policy concerning intellectuals
16. collective leadership
17. individual achievement
18. the interest of the workers
19. to share the same opinion
20. to protect the interests of the people
21. to strive for the right to participate in the competition
22. to draw up a basic law
23. a solid system
24. to change one's opinion
25. occurred frequently in recent years
26. to be taken more and more seriously
27. to believe that all men are equal in front of the law
28. to realize the wish for unification
29. to have more power
30. the folktales that are widely told
31. the cooperation of all the parties
32. to have the confidence and support of the people
33. It isn't easy to be a college president.
34. modern national defense
35. people on both sides of the straits
36. the same social background
37. the pain of leaving one's family
38. the overseas Chinese that are residing in the United States
39. hoping for the early realization of a strong and prosperous motherland
40. Almost all those who spoke at the discussion mentioned this problem.
41. Take as much as you like; there is plenty.
42. I feel that his opinions should be taken seriously.
43. The legislature should protect the people's rights.
44. Did the constitution mention the issue of public ownership?
45. Intellectuals of today are all eager to make a contribution to the country.
46. Only when the interests of the collective and the individual are the same can the country be strong and prosperous.
47. In recent years the government has paid attention to the development of sci-

ence and technology.

48. Only when the legal system is adequate will the rights of the people be protected.

49. Not only can the students of our department attend the discussion on contemporary Chinese politics, the students of other departments can also attend the meeting.

50. How can people's living standard not be high after a country has become prosperous?

第 9 课

谈谈中国的政府组织

谈谈中国的政府组织

（汤姆和约翰休息了一会儿，又接着讨论他们的发言。）

约翰：刚才你考了我半天，现在该我考你了。

汤姆：行啊！

约翰：一九九八年，中国召开了第八届全国人民代表大会。这次代表大会做了两件大事。你知道这两件大事是什么吗？

汤姆：这谁不知道哇？第一件，修改了中华人民共和国宪法；第二件，选举了国家领导人，组成了新的一届政府，也就是国务院。

约翰：全国人大和国务院是什么关系呢？

汤姆：全国人民代表大会既是最高立法机关，又是最高权力机关。国务院是国家最高的行政机关，全国人大决定的国家大事由国务院来执行。

约翰：国务院是由哪些人组成的？

汤姆：每届国务院都有一些变化，不过大同小异。就拿这届人大组成的国务院来说吧，有总理、副总理、国务委员，还有各部部长、各委员会主任和秘书长等。

约翰：国务院总理能当几年？

汤姆：现在中国的干部制度正在进行改革，干部队伍要革命化、年轻化、知识化、专业化。国务院总理一届是五年，连续担任这个职务不能超过两届，也就是十年。

约翰：中国的国务院跟美国的国务院一样吗？

汤姆：不一样。中国的国务院是国家政府，美国的国务院只是美国政府中的一个部，美国的国务卿就相当于中国的外交部长。

约翰：中国政府的领导人叫总理，美国政府的领导人叫总统，可是有些国家政府的领导人叫首相，这是怎么回事呢？

汤姆：这有什么奇怪的？各国的情况不同嘛！有些国家，比如日本和英国，政府的领导人叫首相，因为那些国家还有皇帝或者国王。中国历史上也是这样，从秦汉到明清，每个朝代都有皇帝，管理国家行政事务的大臣叫宰相，也就是首相。

约翰：你还真行啊！

汤姆：那当然啦！

约翰：你说中国的地方政府分几级？

汤姆：我说了半天了，这个问题该你说了。

约翰：好吧，我说就我说。中国的地方政府一般分省、县、乡三级。北京、天津、上海和重庆由中央直接领导，叫直辖市。少数民族集中居住的地方实行民族自治，分自治区、自治州、自治县和民族乡四级，比如新疆和西藏都是少数民族居住的地方，就叫自治区。

汤姆：各级政府的领导人叫什么？

约翰：除了自治区，都叫什么什么长，比如省长啦、市长啦、县长啦等等。自治区人民政府的领导人叫主席。

汤姆：中国有多少省、市、自治区？

约翰：包括台湾省在内，一共有二十三个省、四个直辖市、五个自治区，还有香港和澳门两个特别行政区。

汤姆：你记得真清楚！

约翰：那还用说！

汤姆：上个月我去中国访问的时候，认识了两个中国朋友。一个是北京大学经济系的学生，他家在河南省新乡县七里营乡。一个是中央民族大学艺术系的学生，她是维吾尔族。

约翰：她家在新疆，对吗？

汤姆：对。新疆维吾尔自治区。噢，对啦！今天晚上我还要给他们写信呢，咱们就谈到这儿吧！

约翰：好吧。

生　词

1. 半天　bàntiān（名）

　　　　for quite a while，for a long time

　○ 我等了你半天了，你怎么才来呀！

　　I have been waiting for you for quite a while，why are you so late?

　○ 他好像有点儿不高兴，半天没说一句话。

　　He seems a bit unhappy and has not spoken a word for a long time.

2. 该　gāi（动）

　　　　to be somebody's turn，should，ought to

　○ 我说了半天了，现在该你说了。

　　I have talked for quite a while and now it's your turn.

　○ 这件事你不该告诉他。

　　You should not have told him about this.

3. 行　xíng（形）

　　　　satisfactory；all right

　○ A: 这本书我看一下儿行吗?

　　　May I have a look at this book?

　　B: 行。

　　　Of course.

　○ A: 我一人去行不行?

　　　Can I go alone?

　　B: 不行。

　　　Oh，no.

4. 修改　xiūgǎi（动）

　　　　to revise，to amend

　○ 修改计划

　　to revise a plan

　○ 修改宪法

　　to amend a constitution

5. 选举　xuǎnjǔ　（动）

　　　　to elect

6. 组成　zǔchéng（动）

171

to form, to make up

7. 国务院 guówùyuàn（名）

the State Council

8. 总理 zǒnglǐ（名）

prime minister, premier

9. 行政 xíngzhèng（名）

administration

10. 决定 juédìng（动、名）

to decide; decision

○ 老师决定让我去。

The teacher has decided to send me.

○ 会上作出了新的决定。

A new decision was made at the meeting.

11. 由……来 yóu…lái

to be（done）by...

12. 执行 zhíxíng（动）

to carry out, to implement

○ 昨天执行这个任务的是李明。

It was Li Ming who carried out this task yesterday.

○ 他当执行委员会的主席。

He holds the post of the Chairman of the Executive Committee.

13. 大同小异 dàtóngxiǎoyì

alike except for slight differences, very much the same

14. 拿……来说 ná…láishuō

to take...for example

15. 国务委员 guówù wiěyuán（名）

member of the State Council

16. 部 bù（名）

ministry

○ 教育部 Ministry of Education

17. 部长 bùzhǎng（名）

minister

18. 主任 zhǔrèn（名）

chairman, director

19. 秘书长 mìshūzhǎng（名）

secretary general

20. 改革 gǎigé（动）

    reform

    ○ 土地改革什么时候开始的？

    When did the land reform begin?

21. 队伍 duìwu（名）

    ranks，troops

22. 年轻 niánqīng（形）

    young

23. 专业 zhuānyè（名）

    speciality

24. 连续 liánxù（副）

    continuously

    ○ 他连续担任两届政府总理。

    He held the post of Prime Minister continuously for two sessions.

25. 超过 chāoguò（动）

    to surpass，to exceed

26. 国务卿 guówùqīng（名）

    secretary of state

27. 相当于 xiāngdāngyú

    equal to

    ○ 美国的人口相当于中国的五分之一。

    The population of the United States is one-fifth of the population of China.

    ○ 这本书适合相当于中学水平的学生读。

    This book is suitable for students at high school level.

28. 外交 wàijiāo（名）

    foreign affairs

29. 总统 zǒngtǒng（名）

    president（of a country）

30. 首相 shǒuxiàng（名）

    prime minister

31. 怎么回事 zěnmehuíshì

    What has happened?

    ○ 他本来说来，可是到现在还没来，这是怎么回事？

He said he was coming, but he still has not arrived yet. I wonder what has happend.

○ 她一进门就哭，谁也不知道（是）怎么回事。

She burst into tears as soon as she came in and nobody knew what had happened.

32. **奇怪** qíguài（形）

    strange

33. **国王** guówáng（名）

    king

34. **管理** guǎnlǐ（动）

    to manage; management

35. **事务** shìwù（名）

    business, work

36. **大臣** dàchén（名）

    minister（of a monarchy）

37. **宰相** zǎixiàng（名）

    prime minister（in feudal China）

38. **真行** zhēnxíng

    really competent, terrific

39. **级** jí（量）

    rank

40. **一般** yībān（形、副）

    ordinary; usually

    ○ 我说的是一般情况。

    I am talking about the general situation.

    ○ 这篇文章的语言很一般。

    The writing of this article is mediocre.

    ○ 晚上我一般都在家。

    I usually stay at home in the evening.

41. **省** shěng（名）

    province

42. **县** xiàn（名）

    county

43. **乡** xiāng（名）

    township

44. **直接** zhíjiē（副、形）

  directly; direct

  ○ 他不直接管理这些事务。

  He is not directly in charge of these matters.

  ○ 有话你就直接说，不用拐弯儿。

  Please say whatever you want to say and don't beat around the bush.

  ○ 这件事很重要，你直接去找校长吧。

  This is a very important matter; you had better go to see the president yourself.

45. **直辖市** zhíxiáshì（名）

  a city directly under the jurisdiction of the central government

46. **居住** jūzhù（动）

  to reside

47. **自治** zìzhì（动）

  to have autonomy

48. **自治区** zìzhìqū（名）

  autonomous region

49. **自治州** zìzhìzhōu（名）

  autonomous prefecture

  州 zhōu（名）

  prefecture

50. **长** zhǎng（名）

  chief, head

51. **省长** shěngzhǎng（名）

  governor

52. **县长** xiànzhǎng（名）

  county magistrate

53. **乡长** xiāngzhǎng（名）

  head of a township

54. **包括……在内** bāokuò...zàinèi（名）

  to include

55. **记得** jìde（动）

  to remember

56. **那还用说** nà hái yòng shuō

  it goes without saying

○ A：你记得真清楚啊！

How clearly you remember it!

B：那还用说！

Of course!

○ A：冬天北京比广州冷吧？

Isn't it colder in Beijing than it is in Guangzhou?

B：那还用说！

It certainly is!

57. 噢 ō（叹）

ah, oh

58. 对啦 duìla

That's right.

○ A：这个词你不是学过了吗？

Haven't you learned this word before?

B：噢，对啦，我想起来了。

Oh, yes, now I remember.

○ A：玛丽，你的书包呢？

Mary, where is your schoolbag?

B：噢，对啦，忘在图书馆了。

Oh, no! I left it in the library.

59. 咱们 zánmen（代）

we, us（including hearer）

专　名

1. 河南省	Hénán Shěng	Henan Province
2. 新乡县	Xīnxiāng Xiàn	Xinxiang County
3. 七里营乡	Qīlǐyíng Xiāng	the Township of Qiliying
4. 中央民族学院	Zhōngyāng Mínzú Xuéyuàn	the Central Academy for the Nationalities
5. 维吾尔族	Wéiwú'ěrzú	the Uygur nationality
6. 新疆维吾尔自治区	Xīngjiāng WéiWú'ěr Zìzhìqū	Xinjiang Uygur Autonomous Region

176

语言点和练习

一、由……来……　　　(something) to be done by...

例句:

1. 这个字由我来写。

   I shall write this character.

2. 今天的课由马教授来上。

   Today's class will be taught by Professor Ma.

3. 这个任务由你们工厂来完成。

   This task is for your factory to complete.

4. 明天由校长来介绍各系的情况。

   Tomorrow the president will talk about each department.

解释:

在"由……来……"这一格式中,介词"由"与名词或代词组合,引出施动者。"来+动词"表示要做某事。受事者可以做动词的宾语,也可以在"由……"前边作主语,比如,"由你来担任外交部长",也可以说"外交部长由你来担任。"其格式为:

① 受事者+由(施事者)来+动词;

② 由(施事者)来+动词+受事者。

练习:

1. 回答问题:

   (1) A: 这个问题由谁来解决?

   　　 B:

   (2) A: 这个任务由谁来执行?

   　　 B:

   (3) A: 国务院各部由谁来领导?

   　　 B:

   (4) A: 人民的利益由谁来保护?

   　　 B:

177

(5) A：中国的现代化由谁来实现？

B：

2．用"由……来……"和所给的词语造句：

(1) 辛亥革命　　　　　领导

(2) 办公室主任　　　　担任

(3) 去不去长城　　　　决定

(4) 行政事务　　　　　管理

二、由……组成　to be formed by

例句：

1．这个句子是由5个词组成的。

This sentence consists of five words.

2．我们班是由美国学生和日本学生组成的。

Our class is formed by students from Japan and the United States.

3．这个委员会是由十三个人组成的。

This committee is formed by thirteen people.

解释：

"由……组成"表示由部分、个体组成为整体。个体在"由……组成"之间，整体可以是主语，也可以是宾语。其格式有二：①整体＋由（部分、个体）组成。②由（部分、个体）组成＋整体。

练习：

1．填空：

(1) 这个足球队是由＿＿＿＿＿＿＿＿＿＿＿＿＿组成的。

(2) 中国的国务院是由＿＿＿＿＿＿＿＿＿＿＿＿＿组成的。

(3) 我们班是由＿＿＿＿＿＿＿＿＿＿＿＿＿组成的。

(4) 艺术系由＿＿＿＿＿＿＿＿＿＿＿＿＿组成一个演出团。

2．回答问题：

(1) A：你们那个旅行团是由多少人组成的？

B：

(2) A：这个代表团是由哪些人组成的？

B：

(3) A："晚"这个字是由哪几部分组成的？

B:

(4) A: 由"愿"和"望"组成的词是什么？

B:

三、拿……来说　to take（something）as an example

例句：

1. 拿你来说，就比我唱得好。

   For example, you sing better than I do.

2. 拿现在的生活来说，比过去好多了。

   For example, life today is much better than before.

3. 拿昨天的事情来说，你不该那样做。

   To take yesterday's instance for example, you should not have acted that way.

4. 拿这次比赛来说吧，你们队就不够团结。

   To use this competition as an example, it shows your team did not work closely together.

解释：

"拿……来说"表示从某个方面提出话题，并有举例、打比方的意思。

练习：

1. 填空：

   (1) 依我看，汉字很难写，拿_____来说，就很复杂。

   (2) 中国的名胜古迹很多，拿_____来说，就有故宫、长城和颐和园等。

   (3) 近几年来，在中国各大学学汉语的美国人越来越多，拿_____来说，就有七八十人。

2. 用"拿……来说"改写下列句子：

   (1) 上海在经济上占有重要地位，比如工业，就比西安发达。

   (2) 他每天晚上都学习很长时间，比如昨天晚上，十二点了还在看书。

   (3) 有些方面你比我好，比如唱歌，我就不如你。

   (4) 到北京大学来参观的外国朋友相当多，比如今年四月和五月，就有一千多人。

(5) 他们的汉语水平都不错，比如琳达，都能当翻译了。

四、这有什么……的？　　What's so...about that?

例句:

1. A: 这个句子有点儿难。

This sentence is rather difficult.

B: 这有什么难的，我来做。

What's so difficult about it? Let me do it.

2. A: 这个问题太复杂。

This problem is too complicated.

B: 这有什么复杂的? 我看很好解决。

What's so complicated about it? I think it is easy to solve.

3. A: 你说我写得不好，你来试试。

Since you say that I cannot write well, you try it.

B: 试试就试试，这有什么了不起的!

OK, I will try it.　It is nothing.

解释:

"这个有什么……的"，是用问话的形式，表示与此相反的意思。比如"这有什么奇怪的"，意思是"不奇怪"。"这有什么不合适的"，意思是"合适"。

练习:

1. 用"这有什么……的"改写句子:

(1) 这个问题很好回答。

(2) 这件事不难解决。

(3) 这没什么了不起。

(4) 这没什么可高兴的。

2. 用"这有什么……的"完成下列对话:

(1) A: 我看这样做不合适。

　　B:

(2) A: 我不给你，你一定不高兴。

　　B:

(3) A: 我有一件事，可是又不好说。

B:

(4) A: 这句话很重要。

B:

五、或者 or

例句:

1. 这件事你问小张或者小李都可以。

   You can ask either Xiao Zhang or Xiao Li about this matter.

2. 我想到中国去学汉语，一年或者两年都行。

   I want to go to China to study Chinese. It does not matter whether for one year or two years.

3. 咱俩当中去一个，或者你去，或者我去。

   One of us, either you or I, will go.

4. 或者去上海，或者去杭州，或者去西安，都由你自己来决定。

   It is up to you to decide whether to go to Shanghai, or to Hangzhou, or to Xi'an.

5. 必须会一门外语，英语、法语，或者日语都行。

   One foreign language is required; it could be English, French or Japanese.

解释:

"或者"在叙述句里表示选择。用"或者……或者……"连接两个小句，主语不同时，"或者"只能在主语前，如例句 3。连接多项成分，"或者"可在每一项成分前，如例句 4，也可在最后一项成分前，如例句 5。

练习:

用"或者"和所给的词语完成句子:

1. 请你给我借一本小说，＿＿＿＿＿＿＿＿＿＿＿＿＿＿＿＿。（当代、古代）

2. ＿＿＿＿＿＿＿＿＿＿＿＿＿＿＿到我这儿来一下。（今天、明天）

3. 这篇文章咱俩谁写都行，＿＿＿＿＿＿＿＿＿＿＿＿＿。（你写、我写）

六、我（说）就我（说）　It's all right...

例句：
1. A：明天我没时间，你去吧！

I am busy tomorrow. Would you mind going?

B：行，我去就我去

All right, I will go.

2. A：今天的电影票我买。

Let me get the tickets for today's movie.

B：你买就你买。

All right.

3. A：这篇文章让他写吧！

Let him write this article.

B：我没意见，他写就他写。

I have no objections; let him write it.

解释：

"我说就我说"，"就"的前后是相同的主谓结构，主语多是人称代词，谓语多是单音节动词。这种句型多在对话中表示同意对方意见，只有肯定形式，没有否定形式。

练习：

用"……就……"完成下列对话：

(1) A：今天的课你讲吧！

　　B：

(2) A：你把衣服放这儿吧，我来洗。

　　B：

(3) A：你休息一会儿，中午饭我来做。

　　B：

(4) A：我念完了，该你念了。

　　B：

(5) A：这次旅行让他去吧！

　　B：

(6) A：你不用管了，饭钱我给。

B:

(7) A: 这封信我来写。

B:

(8) A: 我连着演了三个节目了，该你演了。

B:

七、包括……在内 to include

例句：

1. 包括你在内，一共二十人。

   Including you, there are all together twenty persons.

2. 包括杭州在内，我参观了五个城市。

   I have visited five cities, including Hangzhou.

3. 酒钱包括在内，一共五十元。

   Including the wine, the bill comes to fifty dollars.

4. 一桌菜三十元，酒钱不包括在内。

   The whole meal cost thirty dollars, not including the wine.

5. 他把你也包括在老师之内了。

   He counted you as a teacher.

解释：

"包括……在内"大多着重指某一部分（如例 1、2）。有时着重指出的部分可以提到"包括"之前变成"……包括在内"（如例 3），"包括……在内"有时变作"包括在……（之）内"的形式（如例 5）。

练习：

1. 用"包括……在内"和所给的词语回答问题：

   (1) A: 你们代表团一共多少人？

       B: （翻译）

   (2) A: 你们在中国参观了几个学校？

       B: （民族学院）

   (3) A: 中国一共有多少个省？

       B: （台湾）

   (4) A: 你在北京住了几年了？

       B: （今年）

2.用"包括……在内"及其变化形式完成句子：
   (1) _____，他一共写了五部小说。
   (2) _____，我一共买了三样东西。
   (3) _____，中国有三个直辖市。
   (4) _____，一顿饭才花了十块钱。
   (5) 这次只考前四课，第五课_____。

听力练习

(听录音，听力问题见本书附录)

回答问题

1. 第八届全国人民代表大会是什么时候召开的？在会上做了什么重大决定？
2. 全国人民代表大会是一个什么样的机关？这些代表是由谁选举的？
3. 请你说一说国务院的组织，它和全国人大有什么关系？
4. 美国的国务院和中国的国务院有什么不同？
5. 近年来中国政府对干部制度进行了什么改革？为什么要改革？
6. 请你简单地说一说中国地方政府的组织。
7. 直辖市和其他的城市有什么不同？
8. 自治区是怎么样产生的？为什么要成立自治区？
9. 请你说一说现在世界上还有哪些国家实行君主制？谁是它们政府的最高领导人？
10. 请你介绍一下你的国家政府组织。

翻译练习

(英译汉，答案见本书附录)

1. to elect the chairman of the student union
2. to broadcast the election results
3. to form a delegation
4. formed by members of the standing committee
5. to hold the post of the premier of the State Council
6. the ranks of the administrative cadres
7. to come to a decision at the meeting
8. to be carried out by the State Council
9. similar views
10. to take China's situation as an example
11. the vice-minister of the Ministry of Education
12. the Chairman of the History Department
13. Secrtary General of the United Nations
14. the departments under the jurisdiction of the State Council
15. to reform the economic system
16. the ranks of the intellectuals
17. a very knowledgeable cadre
18. to take one's discipline seriously
19. went on for a whole week
20. to exceed the original achievement
21. the visit of the Secretary of State of the United States
22. equal to college level
23. to establish diplomatic relationship
24. the election of the American president
25. to hold the post of Prime Minister of Great Britain
26. Her proposition is a bit strange.
27. an odd incident
28. Maybe it would not take half a day.
29. His skill in driving a car is remarkable.
30. the organizations of the central and local governments
31. the level of elementary Chinese
32. the results of direct election
33. the tribes that lived on the grassland
34. including autonomous regions and prefectures
35. I recall such a decision was made.

36. to achieve great success in artistry
37. After lengthy discussion, they have not yet come to a decision on that issue.
38. This year it is again the time to elect a president of the United States.
39. Has it been decided who will be in charge of this?
40. In recent years, the Chinese government has carried out reform in the educational system.
41. To lower the age of the administative ranks, many young cadres were given leading positions.
42. What is so difficult about learning technology? If you study it conscientiously you will surely master it.
43. Nobody spoke at the discussion, what was the matter?
44. He has been to many big cities in the United States, for example New York, Boston, etc.
45. The leaders of the United States, including the President, visited China recently.
46. Who elected the leaders of the county and township?
47. The ordinary people support this policy.
48. He had been interested in painting since childhood, so he decided to study in the art department.
49. Chinese opera is a very popular folk performing art.
50. This year the production volume in this bicycle factory exceeded that of last year.

第 10 课

在李教授家作客

在李教授家作客

李教授：啊！老朋友，欢迎欢迎！路上辛苦了吧？

史密斯：还好。从美国到中国以后，只在上海呆了一天，昨天刚从上海到北京，今天就来看你来了。

李教授：我们快二十年没见面了。

史密斯：可不是嘛！这次见到你真高兴。你身体好吗？

李教授：谢谢，还不错，就是有了白头发了。

史密斯：我不是也一样嘛。我看你挺好，挺年轻，还不像是五十多岁的人。你回中国以后生活还不错吧？我看你住的这房子就不错。

李教授：这一带的房子都是三年前学校替我们这些教师盖的。房子一盖好，我们就搬来了。

史密斯：这房子一共有几间？

李教授：有三室一厅，其实我们住的房子还不是最大的，还有四室一厅的呢。

史密斯：这个厅真不小！

李教授：这里是客厅，也作饭厅用，另外有两间卧室，还有一间书房，可惜书房稍微小一些。

史密斯：你们的居住条件真不错，不知道现在的工作条件怎么样？

李教授：工作条件也比前些年好多了。中国现在特别重视科学和教育，提出了科教兴国的方针，因为只有科学技术和教育发展了，国家才能强盛起来。

史密斯：记得你得到博士学位以后，我曾经建议你继续留在美国工作，可是你决定要回国，看来你的决定是正确的。

李教授：是的，国外的工作条件和生活条件是比国内好，可是许多在国外留学

188

的知识分子还是满腔热情地回来了。为什么呢？因为我们都是中国人，都想把自己学到的一点知识贡献给国家，希望祖国早日富强起来。

史密斯：这是非常正确的，我相信中国的情况会越来越好的。你们现在的工作一定很忙吧。

李教授：很忙。我们的实验室新添了很多新的设备。希望你有时间到我们的实验室来看看。

史密斯：好哇！要是明天有时间一定去。你夫人身体好吧？

李教授：谢谢，她很好。对了，我还忘了告诉你，她本来准备在家等你，可是因为有一个重要的会不能不去参加，就只好开会去了。

史密斯：她做什么工作？

李教授：在一个中学当校长。

（李太太推门进来）

李教授：正说着，她就回来了。我来介绍一下，这是史密斯先生，美国国会议员，是我在美国留学时的老朋友。这是我太太。

李太太：你好！

史密斯：你好！（史密斯和李太太握手）工作挺忙吧？

李太太：是忙一点儿，甚至连今天星期日也有事。这不，刚从学校开会回来。

史密斯：是啊！中学教育确实很重要！

李教授：现在中国的知识分子不再是英雄无用武之地了。

李太太：你们先谈着，我去看看饭准备好了没有。

史密斯：太打扰你们了。

李太太：别客气，都是老朋友啦。

（李太太走了出去）

史密斯：你们有几个孩子？

李教授：只有一个女儿，现在在清华大学念电脑工程，毕业以后她还想考研究生呢。

史密斯：很好嘛，中国现在是很需要掌握先进科学技术的人才。

（李太太又走了进来）

李太太：你们谈得真热闹。时间不早了，还是先吃饭吧。

李教授：好！那我们就边吃边谈，请这边坐。（斟酒举杯）祝你旅行愉快！

史密斯：祝你们两位健康长寿！

李太太：为我们的友谊干杯！

李教授：干杯！

史密斯：干杯！

1. 教授 jiàoshòu（名）

   professor

2. 作客 zuòkè（动宾）

   to pay a visit

3. 辛苦 xīnkǔ（形）

   tired

4. 呆 dāi（动）

   to stay

   ○ 昨天下雨，我在家呆了一天。

   It rained yesterday and I stayed at home all day.

   ○ 快干活吧，别呆着了！

   Do your work quickly! Don't idle!

5. 头发 tóufa（名）

   hair

6. 挺 tǐng（副）

   quite, fairly

   ○ 挺好看

   quite pretty

   ○ 挺忙

   fairly busy

   ○ 挺有意思

   quite interesting

7. 替 tì（介、动）

   for, on behalf of

8. 间 jiān（量）

   (a measure word for room)

9. 室 shì（名）

   room

10. 厅 tīng（名）

    hall

11. 其实 qíshí（副）

actually; in fact

12. 客厅 kètīng（名）

drawing room, parlour

13. 饭厅 fàntīng（名）

dining hall

14. 卧室 wòshì（名）

bedroom

15. 书房 shūfáng（名）

study

16. 可惜 kěxī（副、形）

it's a pity

17. 条件 tiáojiàn（名）

condition

18. 科教兴国 kējiào xīngguó

science and education can make the country prosperous

19. 方针 fāngzhēn（名）

policy

20. 博士 bóshì（名）

doctor

21. 学位 xuéwèi（名）

degree

22. 越来越…… yuèláiyuè

more and more

○ 越来越好

to get better and better

○ 天气越来越冷

The weather is getting colder.

23. 生物 shēngwù（名）

biology

24. 实验室 shíyànshì（名）

laboratory

25. 添 tiān（动）

to add

26. 设备 shèbèi（名）

equipment

27. 忘 wàng（动）

　　 to forget

　　○ 我忘了带笔记本。

　　 I have forgottn to take my notebook with me.

　　○ 别把这件事忘了。

　　 Be sure to remember this.

28. 本来 běnlái（副）

　　 originally

29. 推 tuī（动）

　　 to push

30. 国会 guóhuì（名）

　　 Congress

31. 议员 yìyuán（名）

　　 Congressman

32. 甚至……（连） shènzhì…（lián）（副、连）

　　　　 even; go so far as

33. 英雄无用武之地 yīngxióng wú yòngwǔ zhī dì

　　　　 a hero with no place to display his prowess

34. 打扰 dǎrǎo（动）

　　　 to disturb

　　○ 对不起，打扰你了。

　　 I am sorry to disturb you.

35. 客气 kèqi（形）

　　　 polite, courteous

　　○ 随便吃，别客气。

　　 Eat whatever you like. Don't be too polite.

36. 电脑 diànnǎo（名）

　　　 computer

37. 工程 gōngchéng（名）

　　　 engineering

38. 研究生 yánjiūshēng（名）

　　　 graduate student

39. 掌握 zhǎngwò（动）

　　　 to grasp, to master

　　○ 掌握知识

to grasp the knowledge
- ○ 掌握政权

   to control the political power
- ○ 掌握规律

   to know well the rules

40. 专门 zhuānmén（形）

   specialized

41. 人才 réncái（名）

   qualified personnel

42. 斟 zhēn（动）

   to pour
- ○ 斟酒

   to pour wine
- ○ 斟茶

   to pour tea

43. 举杯 jǔbēi（动宾）

   to raise（one's wine glass）to toast

44. 位 wèi（量）

   （polite form of measure for person）

45. 长寿 chángshòu（形）

   to be advanced in years；longevity

专　　名

清华大学　　Qīnghuá Dàxué　Qinghua university

语言点和练习

一、……，就是……　**except；only**

例句：

1. 我的发言准备得差不多了，就是最后怎么结束，还没想好。

   I have almost finished preparing for my speech, except that I have not get formed the conclusion.

2. 那个地方风景很好，就是交通太不方便。

The scenery there is very beautiful, only it is not convenient to get there.

解释：

这里"就是"是"只是"的意思，带有转折的语气。

练习：

用"就是……"完成下面的对话：

(1) A：《中国概况》这本书，你都看懂了吗？

　　B：＿＿＿＿＿＿＿＿＿＿＿＿，就是＿＿＿＿＿＿＿＿＿＿＿＿

(2) A：中国有多少省，多少市？多少自治区？这些名字你还记得吗？

　　B：＿＿＿＿＿＿＿＿＿＿＿＿，就是＿＿＿＿＿＿＿＿＿＿＿＿

(3) A：昨天的讨论会开得怎么样？

　　B：＿＿＿＿＿＿＿＿＿＿＿＿，就是＿＿＿＿＿＿＿＿＿＿＿＿

(4) A：他介绍美国的地理环境，介绍得详细不详细？

　　B：＿＿＿＿＿＿＿＿＿＿＿＿，就是＿＿＿＿＿＿＿＿＿＿＿＿

(5) A：你同意不同意我对这个问题的看法？

　　B：＿＿＿＿＿＿＿＿＿＿＿＿，就是＿＿＿＿＿＿＿＿＿＿＿＿

二、替　for

例句：

1. 我妹妹考上了北京大学经济系的研究生，我们全家都替她高兴。

My younger sister passed the entrance examination for the Economics Department in the graduate school of Beijing University. My whole family is very happy for her.

2. 我正要到邮局去，这封信我替你去寄。

I am going to the post office. I will mail this letter for you.

3. 张老师病了，今天的课谁来替她？

Professor Zhang is sick. Who will be teaching her class today?

4. 今天李老师替张老师上课。

Today Professor Li is going to substitute for Professor Zhang.

5. 见到老朋友，替我向他们问好。

Please give my regards to our old friends when you see them.

解释：

介词"替"有"为"或"给"的意思，如例句1、2、5。"替"又是动词，有"代替"的意思，如例句3、4。

练习：

1. 下列句中的"替"字，哪些是"代替"的意思？哪些是"为"或"给"的意思？

(1) 你休息一下，我替你干一会儿。

(2) 我们的工作不同，你怎么能替我呢？

(3) 你能替他画一张像吗？

(4) 他叫我替他请假。

(5) 他需要这本书，我替他买到了。

(6) 旧社会，我父亲替人家干活儿。

2. 从"担心、高兴、着急、管理、问好、去买"里选择适当的词填空：

(1) 见到他，请你替我向他_____。

(2) 他的病快好了，请不必再替他_____了。

(3) 他被选举为人大代表，我们真替他_____。

(4) 在中国历史上，国家的行政事务一般都由宰相替皇帝_____。

(5) 我正要去商店，你要什么，我替你_____。

(6) 明天就要考试了，你怎么还不准备？

我真替你_____。

你不用替我_____，学过的东西我都掌握了。

三、一……就…… **as soon as**

例句：

1. 这句话一学就会。

This sentence is easy to learn.

2. 他一有时间就学英语。

Whenever he has time, he will study English.

3. 老师一讲，我们就清楚了。

It became clear to us after the teacher explained it.

196

4. 他一进来，我就走了。

I left as soon as he walked in.

解释：

"一……就……"表示一种动作或情况出现后，紧接着又发生另一种动作或情况。可以是同一个主语，也可以是不同的主语。

练习：

用"一……就……"完成下面的句子：

(1) 他一下课，＿＿＿＿＿＿＿＿＿＿＿＿＿＿＿＿＿。

(2) 暑假一开始，＿＿＿＿＿＿＿＿＿＿＿＿＿＿＿。

(3) 李教授一回到祖国，＿＿＿＿＿＿＿＿＿＿＿＿＿。

(4) 两位老朋友一见面，＿＿＿＿＿＿＿＿＿＿＿＿＿。

(5) 李太太一进来，＿＿＿＿＿＿＿＿＿＿＿＿＿＿。

(6) 这个研究所一成立，＿＿＿＿＿＿＿＿＿＿＿＿＿。

(7) ＿＿＿＿＿＿＿＿＿＿，就热情地参加了祖国的建设事业。

(8) ＿＿＿＿＿＿＿＿＿＿，我们就吃饭。

四、其实　actually

例句：

1. 他像个三十来岁的人，其实，他已经四十多了。

He looks as if he were in his thirties, but actually he is in his forties.

2. 他以为这件事相当复杂，其实还是比较简单的。

He thought that this matter would be very complicated, but actually it was rather simple.

3. 你只知道他会讲英语，其实他的汉语也挺好。

You only know that he can speak English. In fact, his Chinese is also very good.

解释：

"其实"，说明事物的实质和真相，往往有转折的意思，如例句 1、2。有的则表示对上文的修正和补充，如例句 3。

练习：

用"其实"完成句子：

(1) 你以为他是英国人，_____。

(2) 看起来他很年轻，_____。

(3) 这座山看起来不高，_____。

(4) 你只知道他爱唱歌，_____。

(5) 你觉得他身体很好，_____。

(6) 我觉得时间还早，_____。

(7) 我看他头发都白了，以为他六十来岁了，_____。

(8) 我本来以为他是经济系的教授，_____。

五、可惜　It's a pity; It's too bad that...

例句：

1. 昨天晚上的节目精彩极了，可惜你没去看。

   Last night's program was really wonderful. It's a shame you didn't go.

2. 可惜我去晚了，没见着他。

   Unfortunately I went too late, so I didn't get to see him.

3. 上月我因为工作忙，失去了一次旅游的机会，真可惜。

   I was so busy last month that I missed out on a tour. It's such a pity!

4. 这件衣服还可以穿，你把它扔掉太可惜了。

   This garment can still be worn. It'd be a shame to throw it away.

解释：

"可惜"作为副词，表示对下面所说的事情感到惋惜或遗憾，多半用在主语之前，如例句1、2。作为形容词谓语，"可惜"常见于"太可惜了""真可惜""很可惜"等，表示对上面所说的事情感到惋惜和遗憾，如例句3、4。

练习：

用"可惜"改写句子（"可惜"用在句前和句后两种格式）。

1. 我新买的钢笔丢了。

2. 我很想看那个电影，但没买到电影票。

3. 那个花瓶（flower vase）特别好看，可是被他摔坏了。

4. 我们辛辛苦苦进行了一整年的实验失败了。

5. 这位科学家才五十多岁就去世了。

6. 他儿子学习一直很努力，但是想不到今年没考上研究生。

7. 小王是个有作为的青年，但是身体不太好。

六、（好）多了　A is much（better）（than B）

例句：

1. 骑自行车比走路快多了。

   To go by bicycle is much faster than to go on foot.

2. 几年不见，这个小孩就高多了。

   I have not seen this child for a few years. He has become much taller now.

3. 这几天天气凉快多了。

   The weather has become a lot cooler in the past few days.

4. 颐和园离北京大学比香山近多了。

   The Summer Palace is much closer to Beijing University than it is to the Fragrant Hills.

解释：

"A（比 B）＋（形）＋多＋了"表示相差的程度大。句中"比 B"可以不说出来，如例句 2、3。

练习：

1. 用"A（比 B）＋（形）＋多＋了"回答问题：

   (1) 今天天气比前两天怎么样？（热）

   (2) 他写的汉字比你怎么样？（整齐）

   (3) 这儿的学习条件比你原来的学校怎么样？（好）

   (4) 美国离中国近，还是日本离中国近？（近）

2. 用"A（比 B）＋（形）＋多＋了"完成句子：

   (1) 这儿的天气＿＿＿＿＿＿＿＿＿＿＿＿＿＿＿＿＿。

   (2) 飞机比汽车＿＿＿＿＿＿＿＿＿＿＿＿＿＿＿＿。

   (3) 这个苹果比那个＿＿＿＿＿＿＿＿＿＿＿＿＿＿＿。

   (4) 依我看，这里的工作条件＿＿＿＿＿＿＿＿＿＿＿＿。

   (5) 近几年来，我们的生活比过去＿＿＿＿＿＿＿＿＿＿。

   (6) 我看这里的工作条件＿＿＿＿＿＿＿＿＿＿＿＿＿＿。

七、甚至　even

例句：

1. 他激动得甚至流下了眼泪。

   He was so moved that he actually shed tears.

2. 几年不见，这孩子长成了大人，我甚至不认识他了。

   It's has been years now and the child has grown up. I couldn't even recognize him.

3. 他忙得甚至连饭也忘了吃。

   He's so busy that he's even forgotten to eat!

4. 在大城市，在农村，甚至在山区，人们都常看电视了。

   Not only in the city and country, but even in the mountain areas people watch a lot of TV.

5. 那里不只是大人（会游泳），甚至连小孩也会游泳。

   In that place, not only the adults, but even the children can swim.

6. 他不爱看书，不爱看报，甚至连小人书（他）也不爱看。

   He reads neither books nor newspapers, why, he doesn't even look at picture books.

解释：

"甚至"作副词，强调所达到的极端情况，如例句1、2、3。作为连词，它连接并列成分（包括名词、动词短语、小句等），用在最后一个成分前，突出那一成分，如例句4、5、6。用"甚至"时，句子后面带有"也"或"都"和它呼应。有时，"甚至"和"连"合用，成为"甚至连……也（都）……"的格式，如例句3、5、6。（"连"的用法见语言点和练习"八"。）

练习：

用"甚至（连）……"完成句子：

1. 小张今天起晚了，他急急忙忙跑去上课，＿＿＿＿＿＿＿＿＿也忘带了。

2. 全市的男人、女人、老人＿＿＿＿＿＿＿＿＿踊跃参加了这届全市游泳比赛。

3. 他特别不喜欢运动。他不会跑、不会跳，_____。

4. 这次考试题太难了，不只我不会，_____。

5. 他一天到晚忙着做科学实验，_____。

6. 从前这里是一片荒山，山上没有人，没有房子，_____。

7. 会上的发言要求越短越好，_____超过_____。

8. 这箱子里都是书，重极了，_____
   搬不动。

八、连　even

例句:

1. 连小学生都认识这个字。

   Even elementary school students can recognize this word.

2. 刚学了两年，现在他连中文小说都能看了。

   After studying Chinese for only two years now, he can even read Chinese novels.

3. 他很忙，刚才连饭也没吃就走了。

   He is very busy. Just now he left without even having his meal.

4. 他连打球都不会。

   He does not even know how to play ball.

解释:

"连"强调表示包括在内，后面常有"都""也""还"等和它呼应。
"连"后面的名词可能是主语，如例句1；可能是前置宾语，如例句2、
3、4。

练习:

改写句子，用"连"强调带点的成分：

(1) 他不懂这个字的意思。

(2) 她不会洗衣服。

(3) 难道他忘了上课吗？

(4) 他没做作业。

(5) 他不知道孙中山先生的夫人叫什么名字。

(6) 中国人民的朋友希望中国早日强盛起来，实现和平统一。

(7) 他不懂中文，怎么看中国小说呢！

九、这不　You see!

例句：

1. A：你的汉英词典呢？

   Where is your Chinese-English dictionary?

   B：这不！

   Right here.

2. 他的健康情况一直不太好。这不，最近又生病了。

   He has been in poor health for a long time. You see, he became ill a-gain recently.

3. 他每天都到我们图书馆来看书。这不，他不是又来了吗？

   He comes to read in our library every day. You see, here he comes again.

解释：

"这不"是"这不是吗"的紧缩形式，意思是"这就是"。在本课里的意思是确认、证实前面的话。

练习：

1. 用"这不"回答问题：

   (1) 我的本子呢？

   (2) 你工作挺忙吧？

   (3) 你们每天都有作业吗？

   (4) 你家里客人很多吧？

2. 完成句子：

   (1) 他学习汉语的积极性很高，这不，_____。

   (2) 这孩子整天在外面打球，这不，_____。

   (3) 他最爱喝酒，这不，_____。

   (4) 我认识不少华侨都希望回国看看，这不_____。

听力练习

（听录音，听力问题见本书附录）

回答问题

1. 史密斯先生来李教授家以前还去过中国哪个大城市？呆了多长时间？
2. 李教授和史密斯多少年没见面了？
3. 谈谈李教授住的房子是什么样的？
4. 中国国家领导人为什么特别重视教育和科学？
5. 李教授曾经到哪个国家留学？他为什么要回国？
6. 李教授家里有几口人？都是李教授的什么人？
7. 中国的知识分子不再是英雄无用武之地了，这句话是什么意思？
8. 李教授和史密斯先生是怎么认识的？
9. 李太太是做什么工作的？怎么知道她工作很忙？
10. 说一说李先生女儿的情况。

翻译练习

（英译汉，答案见本书附录）

1. the professor of the Department of East Asian Studies
2. to visit a friend
3. with short and neat hair
4. to seem to be easy
5. a fairly successful young man
6. only in his twenties
7. houses in this neighborhood
8. to be built for faculty housing
9. three rooms plus a living room
10. actually not very useful
11. also used as a living room
12. It's a pity that the room is not big enough.
13. the wish to be a man of letters
14. to pay special attention to education

15. to develop education

16. right policy

17. the condition is steadily improving

18. to implement a major decision

19. to prepare to attend

20. to discuss the educational policy

21. to advocate the spirit of democracy

22. to introduce his wife

23. the spirit of striving for freedom and equality

24. A new style was created.

25. to leave early for another appointment

26. to understand the complexity of the problem

27. only one daughter but no son

28. to have learned a little

29. after establishing the research institute

30. newly installed equipment

31. not to have enough from the beginning

32. a hero with no place to display his prowess

33. to demand the strengthening of the legal system

34. to have a rich knowledge of one's specialty

35. to elect a congressman

36. to be the principal of a high school

37. a large number of scientific and technological talents

38. to master an advanced technique

39. to wish that elderly person a long life

40. How can such a requirement be difficult to fulfill?

41. The tour group from Taiwan actually arrived yesterday.

42. He has always been an optimistic person who is interested in everything.

43. I have no opinion on this matter, so you go ahead and make the decision.

44. With great enthusiasm he went back to his own country to work.

45. He should have gone to school last year.

46. Even those students who have studied Chinese for four years might not be able to read it.

47. Whenever he returned to his alma mater, he always received a warm welcome from the students.

48. Although he is in his seventies, his spirits are still high.
49. As soon as he arrived at the laboratory he began to work.
50. It's getting late, I will not trouble you anymore. Good-bye.

附　录

翻译练习答案

第一课

1. 地理环境
2. 谈谈中国的地理
3. 对历史感兴趣
4. 亚洲中部的物产
5. 物产比较丰富。
6. 内容丰富的杂志
7. 历史悠久
8. 悠久的文化
9. 从第一课念起。
10. 从黄河流域的文化讲起。
11. 长江也从西往东流
12. 全国的人口
13. 全校一共有五千个学生。
14. 研究中国古代的文化
15. 农业比工业发达。
16. 在四川盆地发展农业
17. 两岸的城市工业很发达。
18. 变成一个政治中心
19. 参观名胜古迹
20. 发生了一件大事。
21. 经过努力学习
22. 中游经过三个省。
23. 治理黄河
24. 长江可以发电。
25. 灌溉农业区
26. 肥沃的大平原
27. 大部分的支流
28. 大大小小的城市
29. 山区雨水充足。
30. 像天堂一样
31. 靠着鱼米之乡
32. 海上交通发达。
33. 对交通的发展
34. 对经济的发展起了很大的作用

35. 不只土地肥沃而且风景也很好。
36. 中国可参观的名胜古迹真多。
37. 黄河经过治理难道还会发生水灾吗?
38. 美国人的祖先就是这么生活的。
39. 中国古代的文化是由北往南发展的吗?
40. "文化摇篮"这个名字就是这么来的。
41. 只有发展海上交通,工业才能发达。
42. 大部分的河都是由西往东流。
43. 雨水充足对农业的发展起了很大的作用。
44. 像苏杭一样的风景还真不多。
45. 北京除了是政治中心以外,还是文化中心。
46. 中国文化可研究的东西不只多而且有意思。
47. 最后,我从第一个句子开始再念一次。
48. 难道黄土高原就不能发展灌溉吗?
49. 因为黄河水里有大量泥沙,河水就变成黄色。
50. 像东北这样的农业区中国还有好几个。

第二课

1. 西边高,东边低
2. 由西往东流
3. 地形的特点
4. 介绍中国文化的特点
5. 大部分是高原
6. 他们大部分生活在黄河流域。
7. 发展登山运动
8. 登上第一高峰

9. 试试用中文问问题

10. 小心写错字。

11. 不小心从椅子上摔下来

12. 靠放牧生活

13. 主要靠练习

14. 一首介绍草原景色的民歌

15. 没有机会去参观

16. 四季的景色都不一样。

17. 夏季气候干旱，少雨。

18. 像春天一样温和

19. 所以不适合学生用

20. 草原适合放牧。

21. 气候干旱不适合发展农业。

22. 由于农作物不一样

23. 由于矿产资源丰富

24. 发展能源基地

25. 西部的石油基地

26. 受人口分布影响

27. 影响工业发展

28. 平均分布在每个省

29. 分布得不平均

30. 民歌容易学而且好听。

31. 当然受气候的影响。

32. 沿海的城市

33. 大大小小的海岛

34. 其中台湾最大。

35. 百分之九十的人

36. 雨水十分充足。

37. 多民族国家

38. 汉族大约占百分之九十四。

39. 大约占十分之三

40. 集中在沿海一带

41. 人数比其他城市多。

42. 少数民族分布的地区

43. 内容简单而清楚。

44. 多数国家主要的农作物不是水稻就是小麦。

45. 谁要去中国学习，谁就得详细地了解中国的情况。

46. 不要靠别人，自己先试试看。

47. 由于能源不充足所以工业不发达。

48. 沿海一带人口集中，交通方便，而且工业发达。

49. 那个学校有一千多学生，难道其中没有一个中国人吗？

50. 台湾自古以来就是中国大陆沿海的一个主要海岛。

第三课

1. 暑假生活

2. 放暑假的时候

3. 参加旅行团

4. 旅行团游览的地方

5. 游览名胜古迹

6. 觉得不舒服

7. 觉得很重要

8. 农业方面的情况

9. 唐代的建筑

10. 汉朝的国都

11. 雄伟壮观的万里长城

12. 了不起的建筑

13. 古代宫殿的特色

14. 公元前 221 年

15. 21 世纪开始的时候

16. 相当雄伟壮观

17. 在经济上占重要的地位

18. 地位比别人高

19. 不但有意思而且很重要

20. 长江三峡的景色

21. 海峡两边的人民

22. 山路不但陡而且窄。

23. 沿着一条曲折的小路

24. 内容曲折的故事

25. 有名的诗人

26．工商业发达的港口

27．首都的旅馆

28．一天到晚忙着工作

29．热闹的广场

30．各有各的意见。

31．按照各个国家的情况

32．另外还游览了故宫

33．进一步提高研究的兴趣

34．对大家的帮助表示感谢

35．祝大家身体健康

36．重庆不但在经济上重要，在文化上也很重要。

37．今天天气这么暖和，好像已经是春天了。

38．我第一次吃美国饭是在飞往美国的飞机上。

39．各国的古代建筑都有自己的特色。

40．你知道不知道世界上哪个城市又叫做音乐之城？

41．虽然我们按照他的意思做了，但是他还不高兴。

42．很多学生到中国去一边教英文一边学习汉语。

43．细想一下我觉得还是这么做最合适。

44．这画上的诗是一个古代有名的诗人亲笔写的。

45．小孩儿对什么都表示有兴趣。

46．那个外国学生表示对研究西安在历史上的地位有兴趣。

47．这课课文的内容很重要，大家得细读。

48．中国各民族自古以来都有相当丰富的民间传说。

49．在中国的时候我们一天到晚都得说汉语。

50．休息的时候我喜欢一边品尝好茶一边听音乐。

212

第四课

1．从祖先谈起

2．联合各部落的领袖

3．定居在北方的少数民族

4．形成一个国家

5．形成了盆地

6．常常在沿海一带出现

7．关于西湖的传说

8．关于文字的形成

9．被别的部落灭掉

10．提高技术水平

11．当时反对发展新技术的统治者

12．为了巩固一个刚建立的政权

13．反对诸侯的统治

14．把家搬到中国去

15．果然敌人带兵来了。

16．结果都被杀了。

17．势力弱的政权

18．被灭掉的弱国

19．春秋战国时期

20．古代建筑被破坏了。

21．只好把东西搬走

22．互相影响

23．（他）思想起了变化。

24．商业活跃的城市

25．研究中国古代哲学

26．发生极大的变化。

27．在中央的领导下

28．促进团结

29．势力达到长江流域。

30．参加修路的工人

31．中国历史上的皇帝

32．与其坐车不如坐船。

33．关于他被杀的经过，谁也不清楚。

34．多民族国家的文化是怎样形成的？

35. 农民的生活一天比一天好。

36. 结果一个个都病倒了。

37. 其他民族的人也来这儿定居，于是形成一个多民族的地区。

38. 为了促进交通的发展，那个地区修了不少路。

39. 我以为这个晚会参加的人不会多，结果却来了很多人。

40. 统一语言对促进民族团结起了很大的作用。

41. 互相争权夺利的结果，小国一个个地被灭掉了。

42. 当时的生产技术已经达到了相当高的水平。

43. 皇帝刚把土地分给诸侯的时候，他们的势力还很弱。

44. 孔子不但是哲学家，而且也是教育家。

45. 秦始皇统一文字对中国文化有什么影响？

46. 联合国的建立是不是促进了世界各国的团结？

47. 战国时期各家的思想都非常活跃。

48. 中国是什么时候变成一个中央集权国家的？

49. 春秋时代出现了相当多有名的思想家。

50. 剩下的学生也一个个地搬出去了。

第五课

1. 强盛的时期

2. 力量强大的部落

3. 派兵去打仗

4. 打败来侵扰的敌人

5. 早就有往来

6. 电话打不通

7. 和世界各国通商

8. 用丝绸做衣服

9. 不了解那个政策

10. 举例子说明

11. 流传到现在

12. 原来的情况

13. 原来并不知道

14. 她嫁给一个工人。

15. 发展友好关系

16. 关于水灾的记载

17. 有名的历史人物

18. 哲学家的传记

19. 农民的形象

20. 生动的形象

21. 生动地介绍

22. 既生动又有内容

23. 一部优秀的历史著作

24. 东汉末年的人物

25. 分裂成三个国家

26. 运河上的交通

27. 带来了灾难

28. 代表团的领导

29. 代表全校参加

30. 繁荣和强盛的国家

31. 认识到安定团结的重要

32. 这部作品的优点

33. 反对的意见

34. 越来越衰落

35. 慌忙逃走

36. 中国派很多代表团出国访问。

37. 友好国家互相帮助发展经济。

38. 工厂的领导认识到团结工人的重要。

39. 写历史人物的传记得注意形象的生动。

40. 这个问题的出现很能说明吸取历史教训的重要。

41. 那部优秀的哲学作品写得既生动又

容易懂。

42．早在汉朝的时候就有和尚不远万里到印度去取经。

43．农业发展和经济繁荣有什么关系?

44．请你举个例子说明一下这个情况。

45．他是一个杰出的学生代表,参加过大大小小很多会。

46．世界最长的运河在哪儿?

47．敌人被打败以后就不再来侵扰了。

48．要建立一个强盛的国家必须要发展工业、商业、农业和交通等等。

49．只有靠新的经济政策,国家才能繁荣。

50．去年北方遭到水灾,不过农业生产并没有受到影响。

第六课

1．初期相当活跃
2．踊跃地参加
3．迁了两次都
4．来自北方的外患
5．受到匈奴的威胁
6．解决根本问题
7．解决的办法
8．敌人占领的时期
9．发展手工业
10．把工业中心往西移
11．历史上的英雄人物
12．曾经发生过
13．收复失去的土地
14．首都附近的旅馆
15．著名的宰相
16．一连死了三个人。
17．被迫退兵
18．强迫别人参加
19．分成几个等级

20．促进对外关系
21．节目正在进行。
22．进行文化交流
23．发展贸易关系
24．学习航海技术
25．工业高度集中
26．失去父母的痛苦
27．政府跟老百姓的关系
28．受老百姓拥护的政策
29．结束分裂的时期
30．有作为的领袖
31．采取新的经济政策
32．恢复友好往来
33．制止敌人的侵略
34．为以后的发展打下基础
35．文学上的成就
36．用戏曲的形式
37．大批的翻译小说
38．戏曲在元朝的时候很流行。
39．诗词这种文学形式一直很受欢迎。
40．现在哪一首民歌最流行?
41．这几年以来台湾出现很多优秀的青年作家。
42．在这些问题(之)中,哪个是最根本的?
43．清朝的哪个皇帝先打败了来侵略的敌人,又平定了国内的判乱?
44．农民失去了土地,生活一天比一天痛苦。
45．新的经济政策使商业得到高度的发展。
46．我打了三个电话,可是都没(有)打通。
47．那个地区被占领了不到一年,经济就遭到了破坏。
48．恢复原来的办法是解决不了根本问题的。
49．那个统治者先解决了土地高度集中

的问题，接着又改变了旧的农业政策。

50．一个安定繁荣的社会使青年人有机会作出贡献。

第七课

1．旅行团的导游
2．纪念碑四周的游客
3．对世界近代史的研究
4．掠夺其他国家的财富
5．禁止买卖鸦片的大臣
6．主张和各国通商
7．然后才派兵
8．发动一场战争
9．签订中日友好条约
10．达到平等的目的
11．赶走来侵扰的敌人
12．被禁止的武器
13．参加解放战争的战士
14．十八世纪的工业革命
15．发展社会主义的纲领
16．推翻君主制
17．完成民主革命
18．拥护反帝反封建的主张
19．革命任务尚未完成。
20．临走以前说
21．发动战争的军阀
22．废除不平等条约
23．在集会上演讲
24．在街上散发传单
25．在和约上签字的战胜国
26．支持反战的主张
27．反对的人请举手。
28．产生深远的影响
29．传播革命的思想
30．违背父母的主张

31．排斥反对他的人
32．到前线去打仗
33．终于建立了一个新政权
34．向敌人冲过去
35．长江以北的小麦产区
36．旅行团的导游向游客介绍浮雕的内容。
37．销烟并不是禁止鸦片的根本办法。
38．十九世纪英国商人把鸦片卖到中国去的目的是为了掠夺中国的财富。
39．北方的军阀在旧势力的支持下发动了战争。
40．修缮古代建筑的工作正在进行。
41．签订和平条约并没有制止那个国家发动战争。
42．他从文盲变成了一个文学家。
43．虽然我们已经有了一点儿成就，我们仍需认真地工作。
44．鱼米之乡多半在长江以南，因为那儿的气候温和、雨量充足。
45．孙中山先生去世的时候民主革命还没有完成。
46．中国共产党把老百姓组织起来进行游击战争。
47．参加集会的学生反对政府在条约上签字。
48．新文化运动对中国文学的发展起了很大的作用。
49．成立这个组织的目的是为了促进国际农业合作。
50．我们支持这个主张，可是并不排斥其他的看法。

第八课

1．讨论当前政治
2．踊跃发言

3. 差不多都发言了。

4. 争取参加

5. 不好准备

6. 不同的社会制度

7. 长期的任务

8. 思想斗争

9. 依我看，问题不大。

10. 历史背景

11. 实行社会主义

12. 立法机关的权力

13. 召开第一届人民代表大会

14. 实行宪法

15. 关于知识分子的政策

16. 集体领导

17. 个人的成就

18. 工人的利益

19. 意见一致

20. 保护人民的利益

21. 争取参加比赛的权利

22. 制定基本的法律

23. 一个健全的制度

24. 改变自己的看法

25. 近几年来常常发生

26. 越来越受到重视

27. 相信法律面前人人平等

28. 实现统一的愿望

29. 享有更多的权利

30. 广泛流传的民间故事

31. 各党派的合作

32. 受人民的信任和拥护

33. 大学校长的职务不好当。

34. 现代国防

35. 海峡两岸的人民

36. 共同的社会背景

37. 和亲人分离的痛苦

38. 住在美国的华侨

39. 盼着祖国早日富强

40. 在讨论会上发言的人差不多都提到这个问题。

41. 你随便拿好啦，不会不够的。

42. 依我看他的意见应该受到重视。

43. 立法机关应该保护人民的权利。

44. 宪法里有没有提到公有制的问题？

45. 当代的中国知识分子都愿意为国家作出贡献。

46. 个人和集体的利益一致的时候，国家才能富强。

47. 近年来政府重视发展科学技术。

48. 只有法制健全，人民的权利才能受到保护。

49. 那个当代中国政治讨论会除了本系学生，其他系的学生也都可以参加。

50. 国家富强以后，人民生活水平还能不高吗？

第九课

1. 选举学生会主席

2. 广播选举结果

3. 组成代表团

4. 由常务委员组成

5. 担任国务院总理的职务

6. 行政干部的队伍

7. 在会上作出决定

8. 由国务院来办

9. 看法大同小异

10. 拿中国的情况来说

11. 教育部副部长

12. 历史系主任

13. 联合国的秘书长

14. 国务院下设的机关

15. 改革经济制度

16. 知识分子的队伍

17. 知识丰富的干部

18. 重视个人的专业

19. 连续进行了一个星期

20. 超过原来的成就

21. 美国国务卿的访问

22. 相当于大学水平

23. 建立外交关系

24. 美国总统的选举

25. 担任英国首相

26. 他的主张有点儿奇怪。

27. 一件奇怪的事情

28. 或者不需要半天的时间。

29. 他开车的技术真行。

30. 中央和地方政府的组织

31. 初级汉语水平

32. 直接选举的结果

33. 居住在草原上的部落

34. 包括自治区和自治州在内

35. 我记得曾经作过这么一个决定。

36. 在艺术上有很高的成就

37. 那个问题他们讨论了半天，还没有
作出决定。

38. 今年美国又该选举总统了。

39. 这件事情由谁来办，决定了吗?

40. 近年来，中国政府对教育制度进行
了改革。

41. 为了让管理队伍年轻化，不少青年
干部参加了领导工作。

42. 学习技术有什么难的，只要认真学
一定学得会。

43. 讨论会上没有人发言，这是怎么回
事?

44. 美国的好几个大城市他都去过，比
如纽约啦，波士顿啦，等等。

45. 包括总统在内的美国领导人最近访
问了中国。

46. 县级和乡级的领导是由谁选举的?

47. 一般的老百姓都拥护这个政策。

48. 他从小对画画儿很感兴趣，所以决

定去念艺术系。

49. 中国戏曲是一种相当流行的民间表
演艺术。

50. 这个自行车工厂今年的产量超过了
去年。

第十课

1. 东亚系的教授

2. 到朋友家作客

3. 头发又短又整齐

4. 看起来很容易

5. 挺有作为的青年

6. 只有二十来岁

7. 这一带的房子

8. 替教师盖的宿舍

9. 三室一厅

10. 其实不太有用

11. 也作客厅用

12. 可惜房间不够大。

13. 要当文学家的愿望

14. 特别重视教育

15. 发展教育事业

16. 正确的方针

17. 情况越来越好

18. 执行重大的决定

19. 准备去参加

20. 讨论教育方针

21. 提倡民主的精神

22. 介绍自己的太太

23. 争取自由平等的精神

24. 产生一种新的风格。

25. 有事先走了

26. 了解问题的复杂性

27. 只有女儿没有儿子

28. 多少学过一点儿

29. 研究所成立以后

30. 新添的设备
31. 本来就不够
32. 英雄无用武之地
33. 要求健全法制
34. 丰富的专业知识
35. 选举国会议员
36. 当中学校长
37. 大量的科技人才
38. 掌握先进的技术
39. 祝那位老人长寿
40. 像这样的要求还不容易达到吗?
41. 由台湾来的旅行团，其实昨天就已经到了。
42. 他向来就是一个乐观的人，对什么都感兴趣。
43. 对这件事，我没有意见，你随便决定好啦。
44. 他带着满腔热情回祖国工作去了。
45. 他本来去年就应该上学了。
46. 就是学过四年中文的学生也不一定能看懂。
47. 他每次一回到母校就受到学生热烈欢迎。
48. 他虽然已经七十来岁了，可是精神还挺好。
49. 他一回到实验室就立即开始工作。
50. 时间不早了，我不再打扰您了，再见。

听 力 问 题

第一课

1. 今天，老师给你们介绍了什么情况？你们感兴趣吗？
2. 中国在亚州的东部还是西部？
3. 中国除了地方大，人口多以外，还有哪些特点？
4. 老师的话是从哪儿谈起的？
5. 黄河由哪儿往哪儿流？流过几个省？最后从哪个省流进大海？
6. 为什么说黄河是中国文化的摇篮？
7. 黄河的名字是怎么来的？
8. 黄河现在还常常发生水灾吗？
9. 中国的第一条大河是黄河还是长江？它是世界上第几条长河？
10. "上有天堂、下有苏杭"，这句话的意思是不是说苏州和杭州跟天堂一样美？
11. 除了黄河、长江以外，中国南部还有一条大河，它叫什么名字？
12. 中国古代文化是从珠江流域发展起来的吗？
13. 广州是不是珠江流域一个重要的城市？
14. 你知道，什么对中国东南部的发展起了重要作用？
15. 为什么黄河、长江、珠江都是由西往东流？

第二课

1. 中国地形的特点是东边高西边低，还是西边高东边低？
2. 为什么说，谁登上珠穆朗玛峰谁就是世界上站得最高的人？

3. 高原上的人主要靠什么生活？
4. 草原的景色美不美？中国有一首民歌，说的是草原的自然景色，这首民歌你听说过吗？
5. 冬天，中国北方的天气怎么样？
6. 干旱少雨的地方不适合发展农业，对吗？
7. 中国主要生产水稻的地方是南方还是北方？
8. 由于气候不同，中国南方和北方的农作物有什么不同？
9. 中国的矿产丰富不丰富？煤和石油多不多？
10. 中国的能源基地在哪儿？
11. 中国的人口分布平均不平均？
12. 中国什么地方人口最多？
13. 中国的大城市集中在什么地方？
14. 中国东南沿海有许多大大小小的海岛，其中最有名的是哪个？
15. 中国是不是一个多民族的国家？汉族大约占全国人口的百分之几？你能说出几个中国少数民族的名字吗？

第三课

1. 琳达的信是给老师写的，还是给朋友写的？
2. 琳达放暑假就到中国去了吗？她是一个人去的吗？
3. 琳达是哪天到北京的？是六月二十四日，还是十月二十四日？
4. 北京的名胜古迹为什么特别多？
5. 琳达在北京游览了长城没有？她为什么说长城真了不起？
6. 琳达是坐火车到西安去的，还是坐飞机去的？

7. 西安可参观的地方多吗？其中最有名的是什么？

8. 重庆除了风景优美以外，在经济上的地位也很重要吗？

9. 从重庆到武汉，琳达坐的船经过不经过长江三峡？

10. 过三峡的时候，琳达想起哪两句唐诗？你觉得这两句诗有意思吗？

11. 中国东南沿海最大的港口是不是杭州？

12. 琳达到了上海，住在什么地方？那儿一天到晚都很热闹吗？

13. 苏州离上海远不远？从上海到苏州，坐火车要多长时间？

14. 纽约市博物馆的"明轩"是按照哪儿的园林建造的？

15. 要想进一步了解中国、提高研究中国文化的兴趣，最好怎么办？

第四课

1. 黄帝和炎帝联合起来以后，定居在黄河流域，还是长江流域？那里的土地肥沃不肥沃？

2. 中国人说自己是"黄帝子孙"，或者"炎黄子孙"，意思是说自己是中华民族的子孙，对不对？

3. 尧和舜老了，是不是把政权给了他们的儿子？尧把政权给了谁？舜又把政权给了谁？

4. 为了治水，禹有一次经过自己家门口，只进去看了一下就走了，对不对？

5. 中国第一个朝代——夏朝是被哪个部落灭掉的？夏朝灭亡以后是哪个朝代？

6. 我们现在可以看到的中国最古的文字，是什么时候的文字？

7. 我们从哪里可以看出商朝的生产技术已经相当高了？

8. 商朝最后一个统治者是个什么样的人？人民喜欢不喜欢他？

9. 周朝把土地分给诸侯，这样做，它的政权就巩固了吗？

10. 有一个故事讲的是周朝为什么要把国都搬到洛阳去，这个故事是关于谁的？

11. 有一次，敌人没来，周幽王就叫人点起烽火，他的妻子看见诸侯带着兵跑来，就笑起来了。他的妻子是不是一个特别爱笑的女子？

12. 周幽王是被谁杀死的？西周的国都被谁破坏了？

13. 东周时期，周朝的统治是一天比一天强，还是一天比一天弱？诸侯国的势力是一天比一天大，还是一天比一天小？那些诸侯国是互相团结、互相帮助，还是互相争权夺利，常常打仗？

14. 到了战国时期，还剩下几国？哪国灭了其他六国？谁统一了中国？

15. 春秋战国时期，社会变化大不大？经济、文化发展得快不快？人们思想活跃能促进经济、文化的发展吗？

16. 当时出现了很多思想家，你听说过谁？

17. 中国历史上第一个中央集权的国家是谁建立的？秦朝对中国经济文化的发展起了什么作用？

18. 长城是秦始皇修的吗？为什么有人以为是他修的呢？

19. 中国人民在秦朝统治下生活怎么样？秦始皇死了以后，他儿子作了皇帝，人民的生活好点儿了吗？

20. 中国历史上第一次农民起义是什么时候爆发的？为什么会爆发农民起义？秦朝为什么很快就灭亡了？

第五课

1. 中国历史上最强盛的朝代是哪两个？

2. 汉朝刚建立的时候，匈奴来不来侵扰？那时候，汉朝有力量打败匈奴吗？

3. 汉武帝除了打败匈奴以外，还做了一件什么重要的事？

4. 汉武帝为什么要打通去西域的路？西域的人愿意和汉朝友好往来吗？

5. 西域人特别喜欢中国生产的什么东西？汉朝和西域通商的那条路叫作什么路？中国人是从什么时候把丝绸介绍到西域去的？

6. 王昭君是汉朝的公主吗？为了汉朝和匈奴的友好关系，她做了什么决定？这个故事为什么在中国民间流传很广？

7. 那个匈奴领袖要娶汉朝的公主，这是不是对汉朝友好的表示？汉朝把王昭君嫁给匈奴领袖，这是不是表示汉朝愿意和匈奴友好往来？

8. 司马迁是什么时候的人？他写了一部伟大的著作，这部著作叫什么？

9. 中国从黄帝到汉武帝有多少年的历史？司马迁把自古以来的各种重要人物都记载在《史记》这部书里了吗？

10. 《史记》这部书完全都是人物传记吗？为什么它也是一部优秀的文学著作？

11. 三国时期中国是统一的，还是分裂

的？

12. 隋朝修的运河是由南到北的，还是由西到东的？修这条运河和人民生活有什么关系？

13. 为什么人们常用"汉人""唐人"代表中国人？这跟汉朝、唐朝有关系吗？

14. 唐太宗认识到，人民生活不安定，就会起来造反，这种认识是怎么得来的？唐太宗从哪里吸取了这个教训？

15. 唐太宗还有什么优点？

16. 唐朝出现了很多杰出的诗人，你能说出一两个诗人的名字吗？

17. 唐朝常和亚洲国家友好往来，请你举一两个例子来说明一下。

18. 唐玄宗到了晚年不再关心国家大事，因此发生了什么事情？

19. 动乱发生以后，唐玄宗只好怎么办？杨贵妃是怎么死的？

20. 这次动乱给人民生活带来了什么影响？对社会和经济有什么影响？

第六课

1. 北宋时，经常有少数民族来侵扰吗？这对宋朝是不是很大的威胁？

2. 宋朝打不过这些少数民族就怎么办？这能不能解决根本问题？

3. 北宋灭亡以后，谁又在南方建立了一个宋朝政府？后来的这个宋朝在历史上叫什么？

4. 南宋建立以后，中国的经济中心还在北方吗？

5. 宋朝有一个著名的民族英雄，他叫什么名字？

6. 岳飞收复了大片土地以后，是继续

前进还是被迫退了兵？他是被谁害死的？

7. 元朝是哪个少数民族建立的政权？

8. 元朝为什么不得人心？

9. 元朝是被谁推翻的？

10. 明朝的时候，中国的商业和手工业发达不发达？和明朝有贸易关系的国家多不多？

11. 明朝派谁带着船队到南洋去？

12. 明朝的时候，有没有人到过非洲？

13. 明朝末年，大部分农民都有土地吗？

14. 明朝末年，最著名的农民起义领袖是谁？老百姓拥护他吗？

15. 是谁推翻了明朝的统治？

16. 康熙是不是一个很有作为的皇帝？

17. 康熙的时候，国家比较富强，人民生活比较安定，是不是？

18. 康熙平定了哪里的叛乱？制止了哪个国家的侵略？

19. 宋朝的戏曲和元朝的词在文学史上很有地位，对不对？

20. 清明时期有哪些有名的小说？

第七课

1. 人民英雄纪念碑上的浮雕，记载了中国多少年的历史？是古代历史还是近代历史？

2. 十八世纪后期，哪国商人把鸦片运到了中国？

3. 清朝政府有位大臣主张禁止鸦片，他命令把外国商人交出的鸦片全部烧掉了，这位大臣是谁？

4. 一八四○年，哪个国家对中国发动了侵略战争？这次战争，清朝失败了还是胜利了？

5. 鸦片战争后，中国慢慢变成一个什么样的社会？

6. 鸦片战争后的十年中，中国爆发过一百多次农民起义，其中最大的是哪一次？

7. 太平天国的革命目的是反对"南京条约"，对吗？

8. 辛亥革命的领导人是谁？革命纲领是什么？

9. 辛亥革命结束了中国两千多年的君主制，但是它完成了反帝反封建的历史任务没有？

10. 五四运动是反对清朝的，还是反对军阀政府和帝国主义的？全国人民都支持过个运动吗？

11. 五四运动的两面大旗是什么？

12. 马克思主义是什么时候开始在中国传播的？中国共产党是哪年成立的？

13. 在北伐战争中，哪两个党曾经进行过合作？

14. 一九二七年八月一日共产党在南昌发动起义以后，在哪儿建立了革命根据地和中国工农红军？主要的领导人是哪两位？

15. 一九三七年，日本为什么要对中国发动战争？

16. 在抗日战争中，哪两个党进行了第二次合作？

17. 在抗日根据地，谁把人民组织起来，对日本侵略者进行游击战争？

18. 在解放战争中，解放军先占领了长江以南还是长江以北？

19. 解放军渡江以后，先解放了哪个城市？

20. 一九四九年十月一日，中国发生了什么大事？

第八课

1. 汤姆和约翰是哪个系的学生？是几年级的学生？
2. 汤姆看《中国概况》干什么？
3. 约翰早已把讨论会的发言准备好了吗？
4. 约翰说他要争取第一个发言，这说明他对这个讨论会感兴趣，还是不感兴趣？
5. 中国共产党信仰什么主义？在中国建立了什么制度？
6. 中华人民共和国是哪年成立的？
7. 中国的全国人民代表大会是不是最高立法机关和最高权力机关？
8. 约翰相信中国能成为高度文明、高度民主的国家吗？
9. 在中国，工人、农民和知识分子都是国家的主人吗？人和人的关系都是平等的吗？
10. 中国的民主党派和共产党的关系怎么样？
11. 民主党派也能担任国家的领导职务吗？请举个例子说明。
12. 请你说一说中国要实现的四个现代化的具体内容。
13. 当前中国政治生活中的大事是什么？
14. 实现和平统一是不是中国人民的共同愿望？
15. 住在国外的华侨也盼望中国早日实现和平统一吗？
16. 汤姆和约翰对中国和平统一问题是什么态度？
17. 香港是哪一年回归祖国的？
18. 澳门是哪一年回归祖国的？

224

第九课

1. 汤姆和约翰休息了一会儿，又接着讨论什么问题？
2. 他们两个人是不是用互相提问的方法进行讨论？
3. 约翰问汤姆的问题好回答吗？汤姆都回答出来了吗？
4. 中国召开的第八届全国人民代表大会做了哪两件大事？
5. 中国最高行政机关叫什么？宪法是由它制定的吗？
6. 全国人大决定的国家大事由哪个机关来执行？
7. 请你说说看，中国的国务院是由哪些人组成的？
8. 中国的国务院跟美国的国务院一样吗？有什么不同？
9. 美国的国务卿相当于中国政府中的什么职务？
10. 中国政府的领导人叫总理，美国政府的领导人叫什么？
11. 日本和英国的政府领导人叫什么？是不是相当于中国的总理？
12. 中国国务院总理一届是几年？最多能连续担任几届？
13. 中国的地方政府一般分几级？
14. 中国的自治区、自治州等是不是少数民族集中居住的地方？
15. 中国的省的领导人叫什么？市和县的领导人呢？
16. 中国一共有二十三个省？这包括台湾在内吗？
17. 汤姆曾经去中国访问过吗？
18. 汤姆认识的那位维吾尔族朋友，家住在哪儿？是哪个学校的学生？

19. 他认识的另外一个中国朋友是哪个大学的学生？是学什么专业的？
20. 怎么知道汤姆很愿意和中国青年建立友好关系？

第十课

1. 史密斯先生到中国以后，先在哪里呆了一天才到北京来的？
2. 李教授从前认识史密斯先生吗？他们以前是怎么认识的？
3. 李教授在美国得了博士学位以后，是决定回国还是留在美国工作？
4. 李教授为什么决定不留在国外，而是满腔热情地回国来工作？
5. 史密斯先生以前曾经建议李教授在美国得到博士学位以后继续留在美国工作吗？
6. 为什么史密斯先生现在认为李教授决定回国是不是正确的？
7. 李教授家住的房子是旧房子还是新房子？

8. 李教授家的房子有几室几厅？
9. 中国现在为什么特别重视科学和教育？
10. 李教授现在工作忙不忙？他的实验室有没有新的设备？
11. 李教授的太太是做什么工作的？
12. 史密斯先生刚到李教授家的时候，李教授的太太在不在家里？
13. 李教授的太太是做什么工作的？她工作忙不忙？
14. 史密斯先生对中学教育有什么看法？
15. "英雄无用武之地"这句成语是什么意思？
16. 为什么李教授说中国的知识分子不再是英雄无用武之地了？
17. 李教授夫妇有几个子女？
18. 李教授的女儿在哪个大学学习？学的是什么专业？
19. 李教授的女儿大学毕业以后有什么打算？
20. 史密斯先生赞成她大学毕业以后考研究生吗？为什么？

词汇总表

词 汇 总 表

安定	āndìng	5	（形）	stable, settled
岸	àn	1	（名）	bank, coast
按照	ànzhào	3	（介）	according to
把……比作	bǎ...bǐzuò	3		to liken to
百分之	bǎifēnzhī	2		percentage
搬	bān	4	（动）	to move
半天	bàntiān	9	（名）	for quite a while, for a long time
包括……在内	bāokuò...zàinèi	9	（名）	to include
宝岛	bǎodǎo	2	（名）	treasure island
保护	bǎohù	8	（动）	to protect
爆发	bàofā	4	（动）	to break out
背景	bèijǐng	8	（名）	background
被	bèi	4	（介）	(indicator of the passive voice)
被迫	bèipò	5		to be forced
本来	běnlái	10	（副）	originally
比如	bǐrú	8	（连）	for example
别致	biézhì	3	（形）	uniquely elegant
兵	bīng	4	（名）	soldier
博士	bóshì	10	（名）	doctor
博物馆	bówùguǎn	3	（名）	museum
不但……而且……	bùdàn...ěrqiě	3		not only...but also
不得人心	bùdérénxīn	6		not enjoy popular support; unpopular
不过	búguò	5	（连）	yet, but, however
不远万里	bùyuǎnwànlǐ	5		to go to the trouble of traveling a long distance
不只……而且……	bùzhǐ...ěrqiě	1		not only...but also
（东）部	(dōng)bù	1	（名）	(east) part
部	bù	5	（量）	(measure word for book, machines, etc.)

(教育)部	(jiàoyù)bù	9	(名)	ministry
部长	bùzhǎng	9	(名)	minister
部落	bùluò	4	(名)	tribe
财富	cáifù	7	(名)	wealth
采取	cǎiqǔ	6	(动)	to adopt
残暴	cánbào	4	(形)	cruel, ruthless
草原	cǎoyuán	2	(名)	grassland
曾经	céngjīng	6	(副)	once, before
差不多	chàbuduō	8	(形、副)	similar; almost
产生	chǎnshēng	4	(动)	to come into being, to produce
长期	chángqī	8	(名)	long term; over a long period
长寿	chángshòu	10	(形)	to be advanced in years; longevity
常务委员会	chángwù wěiyuán huì	8	(名)	a standing committee
超过	chāoguò	9	(动)	to surpass, to exceed
朝,朝代/代	cháo,cháodài/dài	3	(名)	dynasty
成就	chéngjiù	6	(名)	accomplishment, success
成立	chénglì	7	(动)	to establish
成为	chéngwéi	8	(动)	to become
吃、喝、玩、乐	chī、hē、wán、lè	5		to eat, drink and be merry—idle away one's time in pleasure-seeking
充足	chōngzú	1	(形)	abundant, ample
冲	chōng	7	(动)	to charge, to rush
初期	chūqī	6	(名)	early period, initial stage
传播	chuánbō	7	(动)	to disseminate, to spread
传单	chuándān	7	(名)	leaflet
传说	chuánshuō	3	(名)	legend, folklore
船队	chuánduì	6	(名)	fleet
创造	chuàngzào	1	(动)	to create; creation
词	cí	6	(名)	a form of poetry writing, fully developed in the Song Dynasty
从……讲起	cóng... jiǎngqǐ	1		to begin with
促进	cùjìn	4	(动)	to promote
达到	dádào	4	(动)	to reach

打败	dǎbài	5	（动补）	to defeat
打不过	dǎbuguò	6	（动补）	incapable of defeating
打击	dǎjī	7	（动、名）	to strike; attack
打扰	dǎrǎo	10	（动）	to disturb
打通	dǎtōng	5	（动补）	to get through, to open up
打下基础	dǎxià jīchǔ	6		to lay foundation
打仗	dǎzhàng	4	（动宾）	to fight a battle
大部分	dàbufēn	1		greater part; most（of）
大臣	dàchén	7	（名）	minister（of a monarchy）
大大小小	dàdàxiǎoxiǎo	1	（形）	large and small, of all sizes
大量	dàliàng	1	（形）	large amount of
大陆	dàlù	2	（名）	continent, mainland
大批	dàpī	6	（形）	large quantities of
大同小异	dàtóngxiǎoyì	9		alike except for slight differences, very much the same
大约	dàyuē	2	（副）	approximately, generally
呆	dāi	10	（动）	to stay
代	dài	3	（名）	dynasty
代表	dàibiǎo	5	（动名）	to represent; delegate
担任	dānrèn	8	（动）	to assume the office of, to hold the post of
当代	dāngdài	8	（名）	contemporary
当然	dāngrán	2	（副）	of course
当时	dāngshí	4	（名）	at that time
当中	dāngzhōng	8	（名）	in the middle of, among
党派	dǎngpài	8	（名）	（political）party
导游	dǎoyóu	7	（名）	tour guide
倒（酒）	dào(jiǔ)	8	（动）	to pour（wine）
登	dēng	2	（动）	to climb（up）
等	děng	2	（代）	and others, etc.
等等	děngděng	2	（代）	and others, etc.
等级	děngjí	6	（名）	class, rank
敌人	dírén	4	（名）	enemy

地理	dìlǐ	1	（名）	geography
地区	dìqū	2	（名）	area, region
地位	dìwèi	3	（名）	position, status
地形	dìxíng	2	（名）	topography
点	diǎn	4	（动）	to light
电脑	diànnǎo	10	（名）	computer
定居	dìngjū	4	（动）	to settle down, to reside permanently
动乱	dòngluàn	5	（名）	disturbance, upheaval
斗争	dòuzhēng	8	（名、动）	struggle; to struggle against
陡	dǒu	3	（形）	steep
渡江	dùjiāng	7	（动）	to cross a river
队伍	duìwǔ	9	（名）	ranks, troops
对啦	duìla	9		That's right.
对外关系	duìwài guānxì	6		foreign relations
夺取	duóqǔ	7	（动）	to seize
发达	fādá	1	（形）	developed, flourishing
发电	fādiàn	1	（动宾）	to generate electricity
发动	fādòng	7	（动）	to launch, to mobilize
发生	fāshēng	1	（动）	to occur
发言	fāyán	8	（名、动）	speech; to speak, to make a statement
法律	fǎlǜ	8	（名）	law
法制	fǎzhì	8	（名）	legal system
繁荣	fánróng	5	（形、动）	flourishing; to make something prosper
反帝反封建	fǎndì fǎnfēngjiàn	7		anti-imperialism and anti-feudalism
饭厅	fàntīng	10	（名）	dining hall
方针	fāngzhēn	10	（名）	policy
放牧	fàngmù	2	（动）	to herd
肥沃	féiwò	1	（形）	fertile
废除	fèichú	7	（动）	to abolish

分	fēn	4	（动）	to divide
分布	fēnbù	2	（动）	to be distributed
分给	fēngěi	4	（动补）	to distribute
分离	fēnlí	8	（动）	to separate
分裂	fēnliè	5	（动）	to split, to divide
风景	fēngjǐng	1	（名）	scenery
峰	fēng	2	（名）	peak
烽火	fēnghuǒ	4	（名）	beacon-fire
浮雕	fúdiāo	7	（名）	relief (sculpture)
幅	fú	7	（量）	(for paintings, etc.) piece
腐败	fǔbài	6	（形）	corrupt, decayed
附近	fùjìn	6	（名）	nearby, vicinity
副	fù	8	（形）	deputy, vice-
富强	fùqiáng	6	（形）	prosperous and strong
该	gāi	9	（动）	to be somebody's turn, should, ought to
改革	gǎigé	9	（动）	to reform
干杯	gānbēi	8	（动宾）	to drink a toast
干旱	gānhàn	2	（形）	dry
赶走	gǎnzǒu	7	（动补）	to drive away
感兴趣	gǎnxìngqù	1	（动宾）	be interested in
纲领	gānglǐng	7	（名）	guiding principle
港口	gǎngkǒu	3	（名）	port, harbour
高度	gāodù	6	（名、副）	a high degree of; highly
高峰	gāofēng	2	（名）	high peak
高原	gāoyuán	2	（名）	plateau
革命	gémìng	7	（名）	revolution
各	gè	3	（代、副）	each, every
个人	gèrén	8	（名）	individual
根本	gēnběn	6	（形、副）	fundamental; thoroughly
根据地	gēnjùdì	7	（名）	base area
耕地	gēngdì	2	（名）	arable land

232

工程	gōngchéng	10	（名）	engineering
公里	gōnglǐ	2	（量）	kilometer
公元	gōngyuán	3	（名）	AD, the Christian era
公主	gōngzhǔ	5	（名）	princess
宫殿	gōngdiàn	3	（名）	palace
宫女	gōngnǚ	5	（名）	a maid in an imperial palace
巩固	gǒnggù	4	（动、形）	to consolidate; solid, stable
共同	gòngtóng	8	（形）	common
够	gòu	8	（副、形）	enough; adequate
古代	gǔdài	1	（名）	ancient times
拐弯	guǎiwān	3	（动宾）	to turn a corner
关系	guānxì	5	（名）	relation, relationship
关于	guānyú	4	（介）	about, concerning
管理	guǎnlǐ	9	（动）	to manage; management
灌溉	guàngài	1	（动）	to irrigate
广场	guǎngchǎng	3	（名）	public square
广泛	guǎngfàn	8	（形）	extensive, widespread
贵族	guìzú	4	（名）	noble; nobility, aristocrat
国都	guódū	3	（名）	national capital
国防	guófáng	8	（名）	national defense
国会	guóhuì	10	（名）	Congress
国王	guówáng	9	（名）	king
国务卿	guówùqīng	9	（名）	secretary of state
国务委员	guówù wěiyuàn	9	（名）	member of the State Council
国务院	guówùyuàn	9	（名）	the State Council
果然	guǒrán	4	（副）	sure enough
过去	guòqù	8	（名）	（in）the past
海岛	hǎidǎo	2	（名）	island
海峡	hǎixiá	8	（名）	strait
害死	hàisǐ	6	（动补）	to murder
航海	hánghǎi	6	（动）	navigation
好+［动］	hǎo	8		easy（to do）

合作	hézuò	7	(动、名)	to cooperate; collaboration
和……相比	hé…xiāngbǐ	1		to compare with
和亲政策	héqīn zhèngcè	5		(of some feudal dynasties) a policy of appeasement by marrying daughters of the Han imperial family to minority rulers
和尚	héshang	5	(名)	monk
和约	héyuē	7	(名)	peace treaty
盒	hé	9	(名)	box
后来	hòulái	3	(副)	later on, afterwards
互相	hùxiāng	4	(副)	mutual; each other
华侨	huáqiáo	8	(名)	overseas Chinese
环境	huánjìng	1	(名)	environment
慌忙	huāngmáng	5	(形)	in a great rush
皇帝	huángdì	4	(名)	emperor
恢复	huīfù	6	(动)	to restore, to renew, to regain
活跃	huóyuè	4	(形)	active, lively
火	huǒ	4	(名)	fire
机关	jīguān	8	(名)	organization, office
机会	jīhuì	2	(名)	opportunity, chance
基地	jīdì	2	(名)	base
级	jí	9	(量)	rank
集会	jíhuì	7	(动)	to hold a mass rally
集权	jíquán	4	(动宾)	concentration of political power
集体	jítǐ	8	(名)	collective
集中	jízhōng	2	(动)	to concentrate
记得	jìde	9	(动)	to remember
记载	jìzǎi	5	(动、名)	to record; records
既……又……	jì…yòu	5		both…and, as well as
嫁	jià	5	(动)	to marry (a woman)
间	jiān	10	(量)	(a measure word)
建立	jiànlì	4	(动)	to establish
建造	jiànzào	3	(动)	to build

建筑	jiànzhù	3	（动、名）	to build, to construct; building, architecture
健全	jiànquán	8	（形、动）	perfect; to perfect, to strengthen
江面	jiāngmiàn	3	（名）	the surface of a river
讲演	jiǎngyǎn	7	（动、名）	to lecture; speech
交税	jiāoshuì	6	（动宾）	to pay tax
交通	jiāotōng	1	（名）	transportation
教导	jiàodǎo	3	（名、动）	teaching; to teach
教授	jiàoshòu	10	（名）	professor
教训	jiàoxùn	5	（名、动）	lesson; to teach somebody a lesson
接着	jiēzhe	6	（动、副）	to follow, to carry on; then
杰出	jiéchū	5	（形）	prominent, remarkable
届	jiè	8	（量）	session
近(几年)来	jìn(jǐnián)lái	8	（副）	(in)recent years; recently
近代	jìndài	7	（名）	modern time
进一步	jìnyíbù	3	（副）	further; to go a step further
禁止	jìnzhǐ	7	（动）	to prohibit, to ban
经过	jīngguò	1	（动、名）	through; as a result of progress
经济	jīngjì	1	（名）	economy, financial condition
经营	jīngyíng	1	（名）	
景色	jǐngsè	2	（名）	scenery
旧历	jiùlì	7	（名）	the lunar calendar
居住	jūzhù	9	（动）	to reside
举杯	jǔbēi	10	（动宾）	to raise (one's wine glass) to toast
决定	juédìng	9	（动、名）	to decide; decision
觉得	juéde	3	（动）	to think, to feel
军阀	jūnfá	7	（名）	warlord
君主制	jūnzhǔzhì	7	（名）	monarchy
抗(金)	kàng(jīn)	7	（动）	to resist (the Jin)
考	kǎo	8	（动）	to examine, to give a test
靠……(生活)	kào...(shēnghuó)	2		to depend on...for a living
靠	kào	1	（动）	near, by; to lean on

科教兴国	kējiàoxīngguó	10		science and education can make the country prosperous
棵	kē	6	（量）	(measure word for plant)
可讲的	kějiǎngde	1		worth mentioning
可惜	kěxī	10	（副、形）	it's a pity
客气	kèqì	10	（形）	polite, courteous
客厅	kètīng	10	（名）	drawing room, parlour
矿产	kuàngchǎn	2	（名）	minerals
老百姓	lǎobǎixìng	6	（名）	commoner, ordinary people
力量	lìliàng	5	（名）	power, strength
立法	lìfǎ	8		legislation
利益	lìyì	8	（名）	benefit, interest
例子	lìzi	5	（名）	example
连（着）	lián(zhe)	3	（动）	to connect; in succession
连续	liánxù	9	（副）	continuously
联合	liánhé	4	（动）	to unite
两岸猿声……	liǎng'àn yuánshēng...	3		Yet monkeys are still...
辽阔	liáokuò	2	（形）	vast
了不起	liǎobuqǐ	3	（形）	terrific, wonderful
临终	línzhōng	7		on one's deathbed, just before one dies
领土	lǐngtǔ	8	（名）	territory
领袖	lǐngxiù	4	（名）	leader, chieftain
另外	lìngwài	3	（代、副）	in addition, moreover
流传	liúchuán	5	（动）	to circulate, to hand down
流行	liúxíng	6	（动）	prevalent, fashionable
流域	liúyù	1	（名）	river valley
旅馆	lǚguǎn	3	（名）	hotel
旅行团	lǚxíngtuán	3	（名）	tour group
掠夺	lüèduó	7	（动）	to plunder, to pillage
贸易	màoyì	6	（名）	trade
煤	méi	2	（名）	coal

秘书长	mìshūzhǎng	9	（名）	secretary general
面积	miànjī	2	（名）	area
灭掉	mièdiào	4	（动补）	to eliminate
灭亡	mièwáng	4	（动）	to be destroyed
民歌	míngē	2	（名）	folksong
民间	mínjiān	3	（名）	folk
名胜古迹	míngshèng gǔjì	1		scenic spots and historical sties
末年	mònián	6	（名）	last years of a dynasty or reign
目的	mùdì	7	（名）	purpose, objective
拿……来说	ná... láishuō	9		to take for example
那还用说	nà hái yòng shuō	9		it goes without saying
难道……吗	nándào... mā	1		Is it possible…?
内战	nèizhàn	7	（名）	civil war
能源	néngyuán	2	（名）	energy resources
泥沙	níshā	1	（名）	mud and sand
年轻	niánqīng	9	（形）	young
农业区	nóngyèqū	1	（名）	agricultural area
农作物	nóngzuòwù	2	（名）	agricultural produce, crops
女士	nǚshì	8	（名）	lady, madam; Ms. (a polite form for a woman married or unmarried)
女子	nǚzǐ	3	（名）	woman
噢	ō	9	（叹）	ah, oh
排斥	páichì	7	（动）	to repel, to exclude
派	pài	5	（动）	to send, to assign
叛乱	pànluàn	6	（名）	rebellion
盼	pàn	8	（动）	to look forward
盆地	péndì	1	（名）	basin
品尝	pǐncháng	3	（动）	to taste
平	píng	1	（形）	flat, level
平等	píngděng	7	（形）	equal; equality
平定	píngdìng	6	（动）	to put down, to calm down
平方公里	píngfānggōnglǐ	2		square kilometer
平均	píngjūn	2	（形、动）	average; even

平原	píngyuán	1	(名)	plain
破坏	pòhuài	4	(动)	to destroy, to damage
妻子	qīzǐ	4	(名)	wife
其实	qíshí	10	(副)	actually, in fact
其他	qítā	2	(代)	other
其中	qízhōng	2	(名)	in which, among which (as an adjunct, with an antecedent previously stated)
奇怪	qíguài	9	(形)	strange
旗	qí	7	(名)	flag, banner
起……作用	qǐ…zuòyòng	1		to have effect on
起义	qǐyì	4	(名、动)	uprising; to revolt
气候	qìhòu	2	(名)	climate
千万	qiānwàn	7	(数)	innumerable (thousands and thousands)
迁都	qiāndū	6	(动宾)	to move the capital to another place
签定	qiāndìng	7	(动)	to conclude and sign (a treaty etc.)
签字	qiānzì	7	(动宾)	to sign, to affix one's signature
前进	qiánjìn	5	(动)	to go forward, to advance
前线	qiánxiàn	7	(名)	frontline
强大	qiángdà	5	(形)	big and powerful
强盛	qiángshèng	5	(形)	(of a country) powerful and prosperous
强迫	qiǎngpò	6	(动)	to force
亲爱的	qīnàide	3	(形)	dear
亲眼	qīnyǎn	3	(动)	to see with one's own eyes
侵略	qīnlüè	6	(动、名)	to invade; invasion
侵扰	qīnrǎo	5	(动)	to invade and harass
区	qū	1	(名)	area
曲折	qūzhé	3	(形)	winding
取经	qǔjīng	5	(动宾)	to go on a pilgrimage for Buddhist scriptures; to learn from somebody else's experience

娶	qǔ	5	（动）	to marry (a woman)
去世	qùshì	7	（动）	to pass away, to die
权力	quánlì	8	（名）	power, authority
却	què	2	（副）	yet, but
热闹	rènào	3	（形）	lively
人才	réncái	10	（名）	qualified personnel
人口	rénkǒu	1	（名）	population
人数	rénshù	2	（名）	number of people
人往高处走……	rén wǎng gāochù zǒu...	2		The nature of people is to move up in life...
人为的	rénwéide	8		man-made
人物	rénwù	5	（名）	character, figure
认识到	rènshídào	5		to realize
任务	rènwù	7	（名）	mission, task
仍	réng	7	（副）	(must) still
弱	ruò	4	（形）	weak
三面环山	sānmiàn huánshān	3		with mountains on three sides
散发	sànfā	7	（动）	to distribute, to send forth
杀	shā	4	（动）	to kill
山地	shāndì	1	（名）	mountainous region, hilly area
山峰	shānfēng	2	（名）	mountain peak
上(中、下)游	shàng (zhōng、xià)yóu	1	（名）	upper (middle, lower) reaches of a river
上吊	shàngdiào	5	（动）	to hang by the neck, to hang oneself
尚未	shàngwèi	7	（副）	not yet; remain to be
少数	shǎoshù	2	（名）	minority
设备	shèbèi	10	（名）	equipment
社会主义	shèhuìzhǔyì	8	（名）	socialism
深远	shēnyuǎn	7	（形）	far-reaching
甚至	shènzhì	10	（副、连）	even;go so far as
生动	shēngdòng	5	（形）	vivid, lively
生物	shēngwù	10	（名）	biology

239

省	shěng	9	（名）	province
省长	shěngzhǎng	9	（名）	governor
剩下	shèngxià	4	（动补）	to be left
失去	shīqù	6	（动）	to lose
诗/诗人	shī/shīrén	3	（名）	poem/poet
石碑	shíbēi	7	（名）	stone tablet
石油	shíyóu	2	（名）	petroleum
时期	shíqī	4	（名）	period
实行	shíxíng	8	（动）	to implement, to carry out
实验室	shíyànshì	10	（名）	laboratory
使	shǐ	6	（动）	to cause, to enable
世纪	shìjì	3	（名）	century
试试	shìshi	2	（动）	to try
事务	shìwù	9	（名）	business, work
势力	shìlì	4	（名）	force, power
室	shì	10	（名）	room
适合	shìhé	2	（动）	suitable
收复	shōufù	6	（动）	to recover, to recapture
手工业	shǒugōngyè	6	（名）	handicraft industry
首	shǒu	2	（量）	(measure word for poems)
首相	shǒuxiàng	9	（名）	prime minister
受……影响	shòu···yǐngxiǎng	2	（动、名）	to have an effect on; influence
书房	shūfáng	10	（名）	study
暑假	shǔjià	3	（名）	summer vacation
衰落	shuāiluò	5	（动）	to decline
摔	shuāi	2	（动）	to fall (down)
水稻	shuǐdào	2	（名）	paddy-rice
水灾	shuǐzāi	1	（名）	flood
顺流而下	shùnliú'érxià	3		to flow downstream
说明	shuōmíng	5	（动、名）	to explain, to illustrate; directions
丝绸	sīchóu	5	（名）	silk
四周	sìzhōu	7	（名）	all around
随便	suíbiàn	8	（形、副）	casual, informal; randomly

逃	táo	5	(动)	to flee, to escape
特点	tèdiǎn	2	(名)	characteristics
特权	tèquán	7	(名)	privilege
特色	tèsè	3	(名)	special features, characteristics
替	tì	10	(介、动)	for, on behalf of
天苍苍，野茫茫 ……	tiān cāngcāng, yě mángmáng…	2		Blue, blue, the sky, Vast, vast, the field...
天堂	tiāntáng	1	(名)	paradise
添	tiān	10	(动)	to add
条件	tiáojiàn	10	(名)	condition
条约	tiáoyuē	7	(名)	treaty
厅	tīng	10	(名)	hall
挺	tǐng	10	(副)	quite, fairly
通	tōng	5	(形)	to open; through
通商	tōngshāng	5	(动宾)	(of nations) have trade relations
统一	tǒngyī	4	(动、形)	to unify; uniform
统治	tǒngzhì	4	(动)	to rule
痛苦	tòngkǔ	6	(形、名)	pain, suffering
头发	tóufà	10	(名)	hair
推	tuī	10	(动)	to push
推翻	tuīfān	6	(动)	to overthrow
退兵	tuìbīng	6	(动)	to retreat; the withdrawal of a military force
外患	wàihuàn	6	(名)	foreign aggression
外交	wàijiāo	9	(名)	foreign affairs
往来	wǎnglái	5	(名、动)	contact, to come and go
忘	wàng	10	(动)	to forget
威胁	wēixié	6	(动、名)	to threaten; menace
违背	wéibèi	7	(动)	to disobey
委员长	wěiyuánzhǎng	8	(名)	chairman of a committee
位	wèi	10	(量)	(polite form of measure for person)
温和	wēnhé	2	(形)	mild (weather, temperament)

文明	wénmíng	8	（形）	civilized; civilization
文字	wénzì	4	（名）	written language
卧室	wòshì	10	（名）	bedroom
武器	wǔqì	7	（名）	weapon
物产	wùchǎn	1	（名）	products
吸取	xīqǔ	5	（动）	to absorb, to draw
戏曲	xìqǔ	6	（名）	traditional opera
细(＋动)	xì(＋dòng)	3	（副）	carefully, in detail
峡	xiá	3	（名）	gorge
下命令	xià mìnglìng	6	（动宾）	to send down an order
先后	xiānhòu	6	（副）	early or late; priority; one after another
县	xiàn	9	（名）	county
县长	xiànzhǎng	9	（名）	county magistrate
宪法	xiànfǎ	8	（名）	constitution
乡	xiāng	9	（名）	township
乡长	xiāngzhǎng	9	（名）	head of a township
相当	xiāngdāng	3	（副）	considerably, quite
相当于	xiāngdāngyú	9		equal to
详细	xiángxì	2	（形）	detailed
享有	xiǎngyǒu	8	（动）	to enjoy (rights, prestige, etc.)
像……一样	xiàng…yīyàng	1		to be like
销烟	xiāoyān	7	（动宾）	to destroy the opium
小麦	xiǎomài	2	（名）	wheat
小巧	xiǎoqiǎo	3	（形）	small and exquisite
小说	xiǎoshuō	6	（名）	novel, fiction
小心	xiǎoxīn	2	（形、动）	careful; to watch out
辛亥年	xīnhàinián	7	（名）	the year of Xinhai (specif. 1911)
辛苦	xīnkǔ	10	（形）	tired
信任	xìnrèn	8	（动、名）	to trust; confidence
信仰	xìnyǎng	8	（动）	to have faith in, to believe; faith, belief
兴趣	xìngqù	1	（名）	interest

行	xíng	9	(形)	satisfactory; all right
行政	xíngzhèng	9	(名)	administration
形成	xíngchéng	4	(动)	to form
形象	xíngxiàng	5	(名、形)	image, form; vivid
雄伟	xióngwěi	3	(形)	grand
修	xiū	4	(动)	to fix, to repair
修改	xiūgǎi	9	(动)	to revise, to amend
秀丽	xiùlì	3	(形)	beautiful, pretty
选举	xuǎnjǔ	9	(动)	to elect
学位	xuéwèi	10	(名)	degree
鸦片	yāpiàn	7	(名)	opium
沿海	yánhǎi	2	(名)	coast; coastal
研究	yánjiū	1	(动、名)	to research, to consider
研究生	yánjiūshēng	10	(名)	graduate student
演讲	yǎnjiǎng	7	(动、名)	to lecture; speech
摇篮	yáolán	1	(名)	cradle
一般	yībān	9	(形、副)	ordinary; usually
一带	yīdài	2	(名)	area, region
一连	yīlián	6	(副)	in a row, in succession
一天到晚	yītiāndàowǎn	3		from morning to night
一致	yīzhì	8	(形)	identical, unanimous
依我看	yī wǒ kàn	8		as I see it
移	yí	6	(动)	to move, to shift
以(北)	yǐ(běi)	7	(介)	to the (north of)
以为	yǐwéi	4	(动)	to think, to believe
议员	yìyuán	10	(名)	Congressman
银子	yínzi	6	(名)	silver
英雄	yīngxióng	6	(名)	hero
英雄无用武之地	yīngxióng wú yòngwǔ zhī dì	10		a hero with no place to display his powess
影响	yǐngxiǎng	2	(动、名)	to have an effect on; infulence
拥护	yōnghù	6	(动)	to support, to endorse
踊跃	yǒngyuè	6	(形)	eager, enthusiastic

优点	yōudiǎn	5	（名）	merit, strong point
优美	yōuměi	3	（形）	beautiful, graceful
优秀	yōuxiù	5	（形）	excellent, outstanding
悠久	yōujiǔ	1	（形）	long, age-old
由……来……	yóu...lái	9		to be (done) by
由……往……	yóu...wǎng	1		from...to
由	yóu	8	（介）	by, of, from
由于	yóuyú	2	（介）	due to, because
游击战争	yóujī zhànzhēng	7		guerrilla war
游客	yóukè	7	（名）	tourist
游览	yóulǎn	3	（动）	to go sightseeing
有作为	yǒu zuòwéi	6		to have achievement
于是	yúshì	4	（连）	therefore
鱼米之乡	yúmǐzhīxiāng	1		land of fish and rice
与其……不如……	yǔqí...bùrú	4		it's better...than
雨水	yǔshuǐ	1	（名）	rain, rainfall
园林之城	yuánlín zhī chéng	3		a city of gardens
原来	yuánlái	5	（副、形、连）	originally, former
愿望	yuànwàng	8	（名）	hope, wish
越来越	yuèlái yuè	10		more and more
运河	yùnhé	5	（名）	canal
灾难	zāinàn	5	（名）	disaster, catastrophe
宰相	zǎixiàng	9	（名）	prime minister (in feudal China)
咱们	zánmēn	9	（代）	we, us (including hearer)
遭到	zāodào	5	（动补）	to suffer, to encounter
早日	zǎorì	8	（副）	at an early date; sooner
造反	zàofǎn	4	（动宾）	to rebel
怎么回事	zěnmehuíshì	9		What has happened?
窄	zhǎi	3	（形）	narrow
占	zhàn	2	（动）	constitute
占领	zhànlǐng	6	（动）	to occupy
战斗	zhàndòu	7	（动、名）	to fight; battle

战胜国	zhànshèngguó	7		victorious nation
战士	zhànshì	7	(名)	soldier, fighter
战争	zhànzhēng	7	(名)	war
长	zhǎng	9	(名)	chief, head
掌握	zhǎngwò	10	(动)	to grasp, to master
召开	zhàokāi	8	(动)	to convene
哲学	zhéxué	4	(名)	philosophy
……者	…zhě	4	(尾)	agent of an action;-er
真行	zhēnxíng	9		really competent, terrific
斟	zhēn	10	(动)	to pour
镇压	zhènyā	6	(动)	to oppress
争取	zhēngqǔ	8	(动)	to strive for
争权夺利	zhēngquánduólì	4		scramble for power and profit
整天	zhěngtiān	5	(名)	the whole day, all day long
政策	zhèngcè	5	(名)	policy
政权	zhèngquán	4	(名)	political power, regime
支持	zhīchí	7	(动、名)	to support;support
知识分子	zhīshífènzǐ	8	(名)	intellectual, the intelligentsia
执行	zhíxíng	9	(动)	to carry out, to implement
直接	zhíjié	9	(副、形)	directly, direct
直辖市	zhíxiáshì	9	(名)	a city directly under the jurisdiction of the central government
职务	zhíwù	8	(名)	post
只好	zhǐhǎo	4	(副)	to be forced to, to have to
只有……才……	zhǐyǒu…cái…	1		only, only if...
制定	zhìdìng	8	(动)	to draw up (a constitution), to work out (a plan), to make (laws), to formulate (methods)
制度	zhìdù	8	(名)	system
制止	zhìzhǐ	6	(动)	to curb, to stop
治理	zhìlǐ	1	(名、动)	control; to bring under control
中心	zhōngxīn	1	(名)	center
中央	zhōngyāng	4	(名)	center

终于	zhōngyú	7	（介）	at (long) last; finally
衷心	zhōngxīn	3	（副）	heartfelt
重点	zhòngdiǎn	8	（名）	key point
重视	zhòngshì	8	（动）	to attach importance to, to value
州	zhōu	9	（名）	prefecture
诸侯	zhūhóu	4	（名）	vassal
主人	zhǔrén	8	（名）	master
主任	zhǔrèn	9	（名）	chairman
主席	zhǔxí	8	（名）	chairman
主张	zhǔzhāng	7	（动、名）	to advocate, to stand for; view
祝	zhù	3	（动）	to wish, to express good wishes
著名	zhùmíng	6	（形）	well-known
著作	zhùzuò	5	（名）	work, writings
专门	zhuānmén	10	（形）	specialized
专业	zhuānyè	9	（名）	speciality
传记	zhuànjì	5	（名）	biography
壮观	zhuàngguān	3	（形）	grand, magnificant
撞	zhuàng	3	（动）	to run into
资源	zīyuán	2	（名）	natural resources
子孙	zǐsūn	4	（名）	descendents
自古以来	zìgǔyǐlái	2		since ancient times
自然	zìrán	2	（名）	nature
自治	zìzhì	9	（动）	to have autonomy
自治区	zìzhìqū	9	（名）	autonomous region
自治州	zìzhìzhōu	9	（名）	autonomous prefecture
总结	zǒngjié	8	（动、名）	summary
总理	zǒnglǐ	9	（名）	prime minister, premier
总统	zǒngtǒng	9	（名）	president (of a country)
组成	zǔchéng	9	（动）	to form, to make up
组织	zǔzhī	7	（动、名）	to organize; organization
祖先	zǔxiān	1	（名）	ancestor
最后	zuìhòu	1	（副、形）	lastly; last; in the end

作家	zuòjiā	6	（名）	writer
作品	zuòpǐn	5	（名）	work (of literature and art)
作客	zuòkè	10	（动宾）	to pay a visit

语 言 点 索 引

好像	3	to seem, to be like
和……相比	1	to compare with...
或者	9	or
既……又……	5	both...and...
(把)……叫做……	5	to call...as...
接着	6	to follow; to carry on; to continue
结果	4	as a result
近(几年)来	8	for the past (time duration)
进行	6	to go on; to carry on; in progress
靠……	2	to rely on...
可(讲)的	1	worth V + ing
可惜	10	It's a pity; It's too bad that...
连	10	even
临	7	just before (something happens)
嘛	2	used with a tone of assurance
没有 A,就没有 B	8	without A there will not be B
拿……来说	9	to take (something) as an example
难道……(吗)?	1	Is it possible that...?
其实	10	actually
前＋[数]＋[量](＋[名])	4	first + NU + M + (N)
认识到	5	to come to realize
甚至	10	even
使	6	to cause; to enable
谁……谁……	2	whoever...
虽然……但是/却……	2	although.../yet...
随便＋[动]＋好啦	8	to (do) whatever (you) want to (do).
替	10	for
为了	4	for the sake of; in order to
我(说)就我(说)	9	It's all right...
先……又……	6	first...then...
先后	6	early or late; priority; in succession
像(跟、和)……一样	1	to be like

248

像	2	such as
要……必须……	5	in order to...must...
一……就……	10	as soon as
一个个(地、的)	4	one by one
一连	6	continuously; in a row; in succession
一天比一天	4	day by day
一直	6	straight; always
依(我)看	8	according to..., it seems to (me)
以(北)	7	to the (north) of; used to show the boundary of (direction, time or quantity)
(自、从、自从)……以来	2	since
由……来……	9	(something) to be done by...
由……往……	1	from...to...
由……组成	9	to be formed by
由于	2	owing to, as a result of
于是	4	therefore
与其……不如……	4	better...than...
在……上	3	on, in
在……下	7	under; with
在……中	7	in; during
这不	10	You see!
这有什么……的?	9	What's so...about that?
整+[量]+([名])	5	whole + M + (N)
之	3	of
只好	4	to have to; to be forced to
只有……才……	1	only...if
……,就是……	10	except; only

责任编辑：曲　径
封面设计：吴　铭

话说中国（上册）

（修订版）

主编　杜　荣（等）

*

©华语教学出版社

华语教学出版社出版

（中国北京百万庄路 24 号）

邮政编码 100037

电话:010-68995871 / 68326333

传真: 010-68326333

电子信箱: hyjx@263.net

北京外文印刷厂印刷

中国国际图书贸易总公司海外发行

（中国北京车公庄西路 35 号）

北京邮政信箱第 399 号　邮政编码 100044

新华书店国内发行

2002 年（16 开）第一版

（汉英）

ISBN 7-80052-854-5 / H·1351(外)

9－CE－3505PA

定价：45.00 元